THE ESSENTIAL

POR

3

1950 to 1965

Your marque expert:
Brett Johnson

VELOCE PUBLISHING
THE PUBLISHER OF FINE AUTOMOTIVE BOOKS

Essential Buyer's Guide Series
Alfa Romeo Alfasud (Metcalfe)
Alfa Romeo Alfetta: all saloon/sedan models 1972 to 1984 & coupé models 1974 to 1987 (Metcalfe)
Alfa Romeo Giulia GT Coupé (Booker)
Alfa Romeo Giulia Spider (Booker & Talbott)
Audi TT (Davies)
Audi TT Mk2 2006 to 2014 (working title) (Durnan)
Austin-Healey Big Healeys (Trummel)
BMW Boxer Twins (Henshaw)
BMW E30 3 Series 1981 to 1994 (Hosier)
BMW GS (Henshaw)
BMW X5 (Saunders)
BMW Z3 Roadster (Fishwick)
BMW Z4: E85 Roadster and E86 Coupé including M and Alpina 2003 to 2009 (Smitheram)
BSA 350, 441 & 500 Singles (Henshaw)
BSA 500 & 650 Twins (Henshaw)
BSA Bantam (Henshaw)
Choosing, Using & Maintaining Your Electric Bicycle (Henshaw)
Citroën 2CV (Paxton)
Citroën ID & DS (Heilig & Heilig)
Cobra Replicas (Ayre)
Corvette C2 Sting Ray 1963-1967 (Falconer)
Datsun 240Z 1969 to 1973 (Newlyn)
DeLorean DMC-12 1981 to 1983 (Williams)
Ducati Bevel Twins (Falloon)
Ducati Desmodue Twins (Falloon)
Ducati Desmoquattro Twins – 851, 888, 916, 996, 998, ST4 1988 to 2004 (Falloon)
Fiat 500 & 600 (Bobbitt)
Ford Capri (Paxton)
Ford Escort Mk1 & Mk2 (Williamson)
Ford Model A – All Models 1927 to 1931 (Buckley & Cobell)
Ford Model T – All models 1909 to 1927 (Barker & Tuckett)
Ford Mustang (Cook)
Ford Mustang – First Generation 1964 to 1973 (Cook)
Ford RS Cosworth Sierra & Escort (Williamson)
Harley-Davidson Big Twins (Henshaw)
Hillman Imp (Morgan)
Hinckley Triumph triples & fours 750, 900, 955, 1000, 1050, 1200 – 1991-2009 (Henshaw)
Honda CBR FireBlade (Henshaw)
Honda CBR600 Hurricane (Henshaw)
Honda SOHC Fours 1969-1984 (Henshaw)
Jaguar E-Type 3.8 & 4.2 litre (Crespin)
Jaguar E-type V12 5.3 litre (Crespin)
Jaguar Mark 1 & 2 (All models including Daimler 2.5-litre V8) 1955 to 1969 (Thorley)
Jaguar New XK 2005-2014 (Thorley)
Jaguar S-Type – 1999 to 2007 (Thorley)
Jaguar X-Type – 2001 to 2009 (Thorley)
Jaguar XJ-S (Crespin)
Jaguar XJ6, XJ8 & XJR (Thorley)
Jaguar XK 120, 140 & 150 (Thorley)
Jaguar XK8 & XKR (1996-2005) (Thorley)
Jaguar/Daimler XJ 1994-2003 (Crespin)
Jaguar/Daimler XJ40 (Crespin)
Jaguar/Daimler XJ12, XJ12 & Sovereign (Crespin)
Kawasaki Z1 & Z900 (Orritt)
Land Rover Discovery Series 1 1989 to 1998 (Taylor)
Land Rover Series I, II & IIA (Thurman)

Land Rover Series III (Thurman)
Lotus Elan – S1, S2, S3, S4 & Sprint 1962 to 1973 – Plus 2, Plus 2S 130/5 1967 to 1974 (Vale)
Lotus Europa – S1, S2, Twin-cam & Special 1966 to 1975 (Vale)
Lotus Seven replicas & Caterham 7: 1973-2013 (Hawkins)
Mazda MX-5 Miata (Mk1 1989-97 & Mk2 98-2001) (Crook)
Mazda RX-8 (Parish)
Mercedes Benz Pagoda 230SL, 250SL & 280SL roadsters & coupés (Bass)
Mercedes-Benz 190: all 190 models (W201 series) 1982 to 1993 (Parish)
Mercedes-Benz 280-560SL & SLC (Bass)
Mercedes-Benz SL R129-series 1989 to 2001 (Parish)
Mercedes-Benz SLK (Bass)
Mercedes-Benz W123 (Parish)
Mercedes-Benz W124 – All models 1984-1997 (Zoporowski)
MG Midget & A-H Sprite (Horler)
MG TD, TF & TF1500 (Jones)
MGA 1955-1962 (Crosier & Sear)
MGB & MGB GT (Williams)
MGF & MG TF (Hawkins)
Mini (Paxton)
Morris Minor & 1000 (Newell)
Moto Guzzi 2-valve big twins (Falloon)
New Mini (Collins)
Norton Commando (Henshaw)
Peugeot 205 GTI (Blackburn)
Piaggio Scooters – all modern two-stroke & four-stroke automatic models 1991 to 2016 (Willis)
Porsche 911 (964) (Streather)
Porsche 911 (993) (Streather)
Porsche 911 (996) (Streather)
Porsche 911 (997) – Model years 2004 to 2009 (Streather)
Porsche 911 (997) – Second generation models 2009 to 2012 (Streather)
Porsche 911 Carrera 3.2 (Streather)
Porsche 911SC (Streather)
Porsche 924 – All models 1976 to 1988 (Hodgkins)
Porsche 928 (Hemmings)
Porsche 930 Turbo & 911 (930) Turbo (Streather)
Porsche 944 (Higgins & Mitchell)
Porsche 981 Boxster & Cayman (Streather)
Porsche 986 Boxster (Streather)
Porsche 987 Boxster & Cayman (first gen) (Streather)
Porsche 987 Boxster & Cayman (second gen) (Streather)
Range Rover – First Generation models 1970 to 1996 (Taylor)
Rolls-Royce Silver Shadow & Bentley T-Series (Bobbitt)
Royal Enfield Bullet (Henshaw)
Subaru Impreza (Hobbs)
Sunbeam Alpine (Barker)
Triumph 350 & 500 Twins (Henshaw)
Triumph Bonneville (Henshaw)
Triumph Stag (Mort & Fox)
Triumph Thunderbird, Trophy & Tiger (Henshaw)
Triumph TR2, & TR3 – All models (including 3A & 3B) 1953 to 1962 (Conners)
Triumph TR6 (Williams)
Triumph TR7 & TR8 (Williams)
TVR S-series – S1, S2, S3/S3C, S4C & V8S 1986 to 1994 (Kitchen)
Velocette 350 & 500 Singles 1946 to 1970 (Henshaw)
Vespa Scooters – Classic 2-stroke models 1960-2008 (Paxton)
Volkswagen Bus (Copping & Cservenka)
Volvo 700/900 Series (Beavis)
Volvo P1800/1800S, E & ES 1961 to 1973 (Murray)
VW Beetle (Copping & Cservenka)
VW Golf GTI (Copping & Cservenka)

www.veloce.co.uk

First published in February 2019 by Veloce Publishing Limited, Veloce House, Parkway Farm Business Park, Middle Farm Way, Poundbury, Dorchester, Dorset, DT1 3AR, England.
Telephone 01305 260068/Fax 01305 250479/email info@veloce.co.uk/web www.veloce.co.uk or www.velocebooks.com.
ISBN: 978-1-787112-96-4 UPC: 6-36847-01296-0
© Brett Johnson and Veloce Publishing 2019. All rights reserved. With the exception of quoting brief passages for the purpose of review, no part of this publication may be recorded, reproduced or transmitted by any means, including photocopying, without the written permission of Veloce Publishing Ltd. Throughout this book logos, model names and designations, etc, have been used for the purposes of identification, illustration and decoration. Such names are the property of the trademark holder as this is not an official publication. Readers with ideas for automotive books, or books on other transport or related hobby subjects, are invited to write to the editorial director of Veloce Publishing at the above address.
British Library Cataloguing in Publication Data – A catalogue record for this book is available from the British Library.
Typesetting, design and page make-up all by Veloce Publishing Ltd on Apple Mac.
Printed and bound in India by Replika Press.

The 356 Porsche was the first automobile to carry the Porsche name. Originally, vehicle production was proposed as a way to offset the profits from Porsche's design business and the royalties being received, as a result of the Volkswagen Beetle's rapidly increasing sales. All told, from 1948 through 1966 around 76,000 356s were produced in a somewhat confusing variety of body and mechanical configurations.

My ●275 356A cabriolet. I thought painting the brake drums black was cool ...

Today, 356 Porsches are not considered to be just used cars, but in the past, they were. From roughly the 1950s through the 1980s it was not unusual for them to be encountered parked along the streets and being used as everyday transportation. They were also not remotely expensive – I bought my first 1957 356A cabriolet for under ●300 in 1971 and drove it home! Okay, it had a VW engine, but for not much more, that was rectified.

This is important because inexpensive, older cars of any type are subject to cheaper repairs and neglect. Coupled with 1960s automotive technology and lack of foresight on areas like corrosion protection, buying a 356 Porsche is somewhat akin to a stroll through a minefield.

My second 356A cabriolet. This one was ●325 and I fixed it!

The purpose of this book is to provide enough vision to make a sound purchase and avoid financial disaster. Unlike more current vehicles, mechanical condition is a fairly minor concern, because in the grand financial picture, even the worst mechanical ailments are generally not terribly difficult to put right with readily available components for relatively not much money. Exceptions: yes, except say, a small block Chevy conversion – then just stay away.

What is really important prior to purchase is researching the authenticity of the model you prefer. This has a substantial significance when determining market value. If your information source is the guys in the local club – even if one of them owns a 356 – this may be troublesome. You'll probably be told that each one was hand-built and that each car was unique, so you should expect pretty much anything. This is fiction. With few exceptions, the 356 Porsche was an assembly line-built production car and changes were made chronologically, as updates were incorporated. Having said that, unlike the typical production car, many of these changes were not made at the model year breaks, but at random times. When you couple that with the fact that cars were not completed in chassis number order, research is paramount.

Most prospective purchases will be cars that have been restored to some degree. Authentic unrestored cars and more recently 'barn-finds' command premiums that are difficult to justify, especially considering the practicality of owning a museum piece. *Outlaws*, recently customised 356s, constitute a genre all to its own. Since they are highly personalised and quality varies, they are not addressed here. Unrestored project cars, while generally honest in their overall condition, are not necessarily authentic and typically priced too high to justify restoration. Restored cars, though, have their own set of problems. This book will help you determine what is the right 356 for you.

Contents

Introduction
– the purpose of this book.. 3

1 Is it the right car for you?
– marriage guidance 5

2 Cost considerations
– affordable, or a money pit?.. 8

3 Living with a Porsche 356
– will you get along together? . .. .10

4 Relative values
– which model for you? 12

5 Before you view
– be well informed 16

6 Inspection equipment
– these items will really help 19

7 Fifteen minute evaluation
– walk away or stay? 21

8 Key points
– where to look for problems 27

9 Serious evaluation
– 60 minutes for years of enjoyment .28

10 Auctions
– sold! Another way to buy your
dream. 46

11 Paperwork
– correct documentation is essential! 48

12 What's it worth?
– let your head rule your heart .. .. .50

13 Do you really want to restore?
– it'll take longer and cost more
than you think. 51

14 Paint problems
– bad complexion, including dimples,
pimples and bubbles 52

15 Problems due to lack of use
– just like their owners, Porsche 356s
need exercise . .. .54

16 The Community
– key people, organisations and
companies in the 356 world .. .. .. .55

17 Vital statistics
– essential data at your fingertips .. .57

Index 64

THE ESSENTIAL BUYER'S GUIDE™ CURRENCY
At the time of publication a BG unit of currency "●" equals approximately
US$1.00/£0.76/Euro 0.85. Please adjust to suit current exchange rates using
US$ as the base currency.

1 Is it the right car for you?
– marriage guidance

Tall and short drivers
Compared with similar era sports cars, 356 Porsches are surprisingly accommodating for taller drivers.

Weight of controls
Stated here for the first of many times: newer models are better than older ones in most of these areas due to constant upgrading of components. A 356C will require less steering effort and braking effort than earlier models, and have superior gear change.

Will it fit in the garage?
356s are small cars and fit in just about any garage. Perhaps, a better question is: Do you have a climate-controlled garage?

Interior space
For a sports car the front seat area is reasonably spacious, with a very low centre tunnel. The back seat area, though, is best used for small children only.

Compared to its contemporaries, the 356 had wide seats and loads of leg room.

On early cars precious little space for luggage up front can be a problem, though there is room behind the seats, and a rear luggage rack can help offset this.

Luggage capacity

In earlier cars (through 1961), the fuel tank and spare tyre leave very little storage room up front. A small toolbox and a proper jack are good choices. Later cars have a bit more room. With the rear seats folded, a couple of sensibly sized luggage items can be stowed and brackets for straps are provided on all but the very first cars. In addition rear lid-mounted luggage racks were a frequently fitted factory option along with being period accessories.

Running costs

Since a 356 is not typically used as a daily driver, running costs are largely irrelevant. A larger concern is fuel availability. While all 356s will happily run on unleaded gasoline with a reasonable octane rating, ethanol content is a concern for later cars with plastic carburettor floats. As with most early air-cooled cars, oil consumption is higher than with modern cars.

Usability

356s are quite drivable cars, even the early models. They are not practical for daily use, due to their vulnerability to casual damage. Inclement weather is also not a strong suit for the 356. You might want to invest in some Rain-X to assist the tiny wiper blades or if you have an open car, especially a Speedster, it is probably best to leave it in that climate-controlled garage. Speaking of heat, the air-cooled engine also did not do a very good job of heating the interior, so even if it is dry, when it's cold, keep it in that garage.

Parts availability

The 356 Porsche is a simple car. It also shares some mechanical components with period VWs. In the 1970s the aftermarket began to manufacture replacement parts, and continues to do so. Porsche AG also joined the game at a later date. Many of the manufacturers of replacement mechanical and electrical items, just never stopped making them. Additional OEM (original equipment manufacturer) suppliers have been encouraged to remanufacture even more obscure items. Authenticity is cherished by the market, and some replacement items require a little, to quite a bit, of help to look and fit correctly.

Parts cost

Prices are all over the place. The new to market, more obscure items are typically pretty pricey. Some items like rubber seals actually have multiple aftermarket manufacturers – and OEM in this area may or may not be better. Consult the clubs. Used original parts are still out there and are sometimes amazing bargains – or not. Due diligence here is in order.

Insurance

Classic car insurance in the US is amazingly affordable, and, for the most part, restrictions on use are not a concern. They also routinely provide customer service that is superlative. In the rest of the world, we're back to due diligence. Hopefully, the American model will prevail.

Investment potential

Forty years ago, when 356s were around £1000 in *Exchange & Mart*, would have been a good time to buy several. I bought a '65 911 for £400 – should have bought more. The incredible appreciation rate in recent years will stop at some point, and just like Model T Fords, they'll head back down. Buyers of more pedestrian models will be less enthused as they get older. Rare models, on the other hand, will just keep going up – like say, Duesenbergs. Best recommendation is buy what you want; don't buy a future collectible.

Foibles

Hey, it's an old car. It doesn't handle like a modern car. Don't drive it like a crazy person or it may back around through the turn and cause grave body damage. With the exception of 356C models, it actually won't stop like a modern car – and no 356s originally had the benefit of dual brake system. More later.

Plus points

They are real Porsches and look a lot like Easter eggs. People at the gas station will marvel about opening the front lid before fueling. Don't let attendants help – ever!

Minus points

They are really old and somewhat fragile. You can't park and leave them just anywhere. Don't want to be driven in inclement weather.

Alternatives

Mercedes Benz 190 SL, Jaguar XKs, Big Healeys.

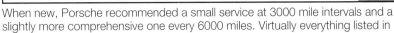

2 Cost considerations
– affordable, or a money pit?

When new, Porsche recommended a small service at 3000 mile intervals and a slightly more comprehensive one every 6000 miles. Virtually everything listed in these services can be easily done by the mechanically-oriented owner. If you choose to have any mechanical work done professionally, you are best served by utilizing specialists who are familiar with 356s.

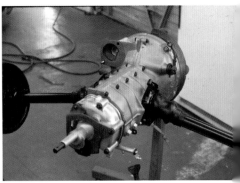

A gearbox rebuild can be an expensive proposition. Thankfully specialist firms have reproduced many of the needed components.

3000 mile service cost, including parts:
● 650–1000
6000 mile service cost, including parts:
● 700–1100

Since area labour rates vary significantly, the following are listed in hours. Also be aware that as cars become older, repair may be more costly due to replacement of increasingly difficult to find components: courtesy European Performance and Zims Autotecknik

Engine rebuild: 20–40 hours (not including valve job)
Gearbox rebuild: 7–15 hours (additional time if ring and pinion needs attention)
Clutch installation: 3–8 hours
Front end rebuild (king and link pin replacement): 4–12 hours (not including alignment)
Carb rebuild: 4–6 hours (more for throttle shaft wear and thread damage)

Mechanical parts cost
Due to the differences in specifications over the years, some of these have widely varying cost. To help keep things simple, we have eliminated four-cam models and other exotica. Prices were accurate at date of publication: courtesy Brad Ripley

Engine rebuild: ● 7500–9000
Gearbox rebuild: ● 4500–5500
New clutch: ● 510
Brake drum, front 1953–1963: new ● 1800; rebuilt ● 600
Brake drum, rear 1953–1963: new ● 1800; rebuilt ● 600
Brake shoe set (four wheels): ● 350
Wheel cylinder (each): ● 45
Brake rotor, front 1964–1965: ● 50
Brake rotor, rear 1964–1965: ● 90
Brake pad set (four wheels): ● 160

Brake master cylinder: drum ●110; disc ●170
Front suspension king and link pin repair set: ●295
Muffler: ●540
Heat exchanger: ●345
Tune up parts: ●150
Carburettor rebuild kits: ●80 (for 2 carburettors)
Fuel pump rebuild kits: ●35
Dampers, front (pair): Boge ●120
Dampers, rear (pair): Boge ●120

Exterior trim
Headlight: ●110
Taillight: teardrop ●90
Bumper trim, deco trim and guards (1
bumper): ●650–775

Upholstery
Carpet set: ●900
Upholstery set, vinyl: ●750
Upholstery set, leather: ●4000
Front rubber floor mat: ●260
Convertible top: including cabriolet
headliner ●950–1390

Structural repair and paint cost can
make any 356 a risky proposition. Not
this one, though: it turned out just fine
(see photo in chapter head).

Manuals
Workshop manual: new factory
reprint ●350
Owner's manual: new factory reprint ●100

Structural repair
Also varies tremendously based on condition of the car. Despite the availability of
replacement parts, repair of extensively rusty or damaged examples can only be
justified if the acquisition price is low, model is rare or for sentimental reasons.

Complete structural repair: ●30,000–80,000+
Professional respray including basic prep: ●10,000–15,000

Parts that are easy to find
Because of the high prices that 356s bring, the vast majority of parts are available
on the aftermarket, including items produced by the original manufacturers, even
Porsche. Some are absolutely spot-on and others less so.

Parts that are hard to find
Items that are not reproduced such as radios, some obscure mechanical/trim parts
and formerly plentiful NOS (new old stock) pieces.

Parts that are very expensive
NOS and good original interior trim parts and lights for discriminating owners. Also
parts for really early and four-cam cars.

3 Living with a Porsche 356
– will you get along together?

There was a time when 356s were reasonably priced transportation for people without children. Regrettably, that was 50 years ago. Now, they are high-priced toys for the same demographic. Most models are still quite capable in terms of being fun to drive and keeping up with modern traffic, but they have only the practicality and sophistication of vehicles from the 1950s and '60s – ie no electronics, no cruise control, no air-conditioning.

The first prerequisites are to have garage space and a real car. 356s are decidedly no longer considered all-weather cars. While period Porsche photos show ecstatic motorists waist-deep in snow standing by their 356s with skis strapped to the rear-mounted luggage racks, there are no first person interviews about the marvellous performance of the heater and defroster. Defogging and wiper performance are equally dismal, though there are modern chemical solutions thanks to the folks at Rain-X.

With the exception of four-cam cars, performance is decidedly pedestrian. The fastest 0–60mph acceleration recorded by period magazines was well north of ten seconds with top speeds under 100mph (or much lower, depending on engine fitted and gearing), though the optimistic reading speedometers will make you feel better.

The earlier the car, the more leisurely you should be stirring the shift lever. Through 1952, there were no synchronisers. In 1953, Porsche introduced its own synchronisers and they were better. By the autumn of 1958 superior blocking synchromesh was introduced with the 716 gearbox, which resolved this weakness.

Driving your open car in the snow with the top folded is not all that much different from driving a coupe, as far as interior temperature is concerned. Why are these people smiling? (Courtesy Porsche AG)

The large 11in four-wheel aluminium drum brakes first fitted for the 1953 model year are more than adequate, and the disc brakes fitted to the 356C were a step better. Steering also took a giant leap from the original VW box to one supplied by ZF beginning at the 1958 model year.

If not already equipped, for a

Since no temperature gauge is present it means this 356 is no later than early 1951. The most powerful engine available at that time produced 44hp, yet this car is traveling at 140kph (87mph). An early example of the optimistic Porsche 356 speedometer. (Courtesy Porsche AG)

modest sum, put a set of modern (or classic) radial tyres on it – full aspect, or it won't look right. If earlier than 1956, there are no radials at this time that fit the 3.25x16in rims.

The take home message here is obvious: the more recent the 356, the more like modern cars it will be. The newest 356C is still over 50 years old, though.

The age factor can also be a plus. If you are remotely mechanical, all 356s provide a straightforward, uncomplicated platform for maintenance and repairs. They were well engineered and assembled at a very high standard, making them a pleasure to experience when well maintained.

All this quality, of course, came and now comes at a price. Entry level for a driver quality bottom of the line 356B is roughly ●35K, or up that to about ●300K for a Speedster, add a four-cam engine and add around a million – but at least it won't be driver quality, because there aren't any. So, if you want to live with a 356, be financially prepared.

Back to driving – mileage and noise levels are not so impressive, but should be okay for most. Droning at constant speed on road trips can be a bit trying, especially if equipped with the sport exhaust or aftermarket performance muffler. Fuel economy? Remember, you paid a small fortune for the car.

Speaking of road trips, open cars can be fun and while wet weather protection is generally respectable, Speedsters make a great case for the use of enclosed trailers. Oh, and don't forget to carry along appropriate tools and spares. You won't find many 356 bits at Halfords or NAPA.

If it is really hot, you'll need to invest in a pair of those nifty 1950s era leather driving gloves with the open knuckles. Without them, you won't be able to hold on to the plastic steering wheel.

Then, there is not driving it, which is also a concern. If you leave it parked for too long, the mechanical components begin to break down and eventually can require major rehab. So, routine exercise is required. Having said that, you really can't just get in and pop down to the grocery – unless you park a block away. Even then, there are inherent risks leaving it to fend for itself.

Still, it is fun to look at it in the garage and drive down winding roads just before sunset. Regrettably, when it gets dark, the 6-volt headlights only provide kind of a ghostly yellow glow. Go back and look at it in the garage and congratulate yourself on your good taste.

A safe place to drive your 356 is at Porsche club driving (not track) events. Unless exclusively for 356s, you'll have the only car this old, and will probably struggle to keep up with the others.

4 Relative values
– which model for you?

Chronologically, there are four distinct 356 models that cover the 1950 through 1965 model years. With the exception of the 356C, all other models have at least three distinct body types and a number of different engine options. What you want can be based on which one you like best, identify with, lust after or can afford.

356, 1950–1955: the first production cars

An incredible amount of evolution occurs within this model range. The earliest cars are really best suited for museums, with their low power, unsynchronised gearboxes, narrow wheels and VW brakes. The original smooth aerodynamic design was gradually altered, occasionally awkwardly, but mechanical advances through the range, made 356s from 1953 reasonably drivable. Best evaluation of them is quirky.

Coupe and cabriolet models were available right from the start, with the inexpensive Speedster model introduced for the 1955 model year, primarily for consumption in the US market. Some early cabriolets were produced by the coachbuilder Gläser, which went into receivership before completing its 1952 contract. All other 356s were built by the neighbourhood coachbuilder, Reutter Karosserie.

Also introduced during the 1955 model year was the exotic four-cam Carrera engine. It was fitted to only a small number of coupes and Speedsters.

356A, 1956–1959: the pretty ones

The curved windshields and a little more brightwork made the 356A arguably the best looking 356. Coupe, cabriolet and Speedster models continued with fewer Speedsters built every year, stopping with just a handful in 1959. A more civilised Convertible D with

1951 Gläser-bodied cabriolet.

1952 Reutter-bodied cabriolet. (Courtesy Porsche AG)

The very rare aluminium-bodied America Roadster was built in 1951 and 1952 by Gläser. You can't afford one.

356 Speedster flanked by 1956 356A coupe. (Courtesy Porsche AG)

taller windshield (windscreen) and roll-up side windows was introduced as a Speedster replacement midway through the 1958 model year. It was outsourced to the coachbuilder Drauz in Germany.

Smaller diameter wheels were also over an inch wider than those fitted to the earlier cars. Rear suspension design was also radically improved, making the 356A a much more sporty and comfortable car to drive.

A division within the 356A model occurred between the 1957 and 1958 model years. The later cars are referred to as T 2s, which stood for Technical Program 2. They have some body modifications, including a removable hardtop for cabriolets, and the superior ZF steering box. The upgraded 716 gearbox was a mid-year change in 1958.

Carrera engines in multiple versions were fitted to all models during this era, and these cars are among the most expensive 356s today.

356B 1960–1963: time for a change

Pressured by regulations and distributors, the 356B maintained a family resemblance to earlier cars, but had much higher headlights and beefier bumpers. The Roadster replaced the Convertible D, but was basically the same concept. During 1961 the Karmann Hardtop aka (Notchback) was introduced. It resembled a cabriolet with a hardtop, but the top did not come off. It was another outsourced model, this time to coachbuilder Karmann, hence the name. Today, despite being quite rare, it represents the least valuable 356 available.

Like the 356A, there were two varieties of 356Bs: the T 5 and the T 6. This change occurred between the 1961 and 1962 model years, and resulted

The 356B Roadster, the last of the lightweight open cars. (Courtesy Bill Perrone)

The unloved Karmann Hardtop.
(Courtesy Steve Moore)

in a very different looking car. The T 6 was the first 356 with an external gas filler, eliminating the chance of inflicting damage while filling the tank.

The front lid was squared off up front and the area below redesigned, yielding substantially more luggage space. The rear lid sprouted an extra rear grille, and the coupe lid and rear glass were substantially larger.

Both Roadster and Karmann Hardtop made the transition to the T 6, but just barely. Under 700 Hardtops were constructed and only 249 of the dual grille Roadsters rolled off the assembly line at d'leteren in Belgium, who took over from Drauz in mid-1961.

Karmann, on the other hand, happily transitioned to making standard shaped coupes, and continued to make them through the end of 356 production in 1965. 356 folks tend to prefer the Reutter ones.

The T 6 356B Carrera 2 had Porsche designed annular disc brakes, which gave way to conventional discs on the 356C. (Courtesy Jack Arct)

The exotic four-cam engine all but disappeared for a while, but returned during T 6 production as the sophisticated Carrera 2 model, so named for its two litre displacement. Some of these were fitted with the unusual Porsche-designed annular disc brakes.

356C 1964–1965: end of the line

Coupe and cabriolet models continued with coachbuilder Reutter being absorbed by Porsche in December of 1963. Reutter lived on as a spinoff company named Recaro that continues to manufacture seats.

The main improvement of the 356C was the adoption of disc brakes manufactured by Ate under license. These were also used on the 356C-based Carrera 2. There was little else new, as the folks in Zuffenhausen were gearing up for production of the 911.

A run of ten cabriolets was specially constructed in March of 1966 for the Dutch police, who wanted open cars. Some of these are still out there.

Probably the best choice, if you want a 356 to drive in nice climates: the 356C cabriolet. (Courtesy Dennis Frick)

Relative values

356s come in many varieties, but the most common body style of all years is the coupe equipped with the least tuned engine type, referred to as Normals or Damen (ladies). For this exercise, we will assign 100% to the value of a 356A coupe equipped with a 1600 Normal powerplant. Values are also based on high quality driver 356s. Concours level cars will be between 50% and 100% higher across the board.

For actual current market prices, I'd recommend the valuation tool at www.hagerty.com. It is free and values are derived not only from auction sales, but private ones as well.

356
1951–1955 coupe **80%**, 1951 **180%**, 1500S engine **150%**
1951–1955 cabriolet **150%**, 1951 **350%**, 1500S engine **250%**
1955 Speedster **400%**, 1500S engine **450%**, four-cam **1500%**

356A
1956–1957 coupe **100%**, 1600S engine **160%**, four-cam GS **750%** four-cam GS/GT **900%**
1958–1959 coupe **110%**, 1600S engine **160%**, four-cam GS **750%** four-cam GS/GT **1500%**
1956–1959 cabriolet **180%**, 1600S engine **240%**, four-cam GS **1400%**
1956–1957 Speedster **300%**, 1600S engine **430%**, four-cam GS **1500%**, four-cam GS/GT **1800%**
1958–1959 Speedster **400%**, 1600S engine **440%**, four-cam GS **1600%**, four-cam GS/GT **2000%**
1958–1959 Convertible D **240%**, 1600S engine **300%**

356B
1960–1961 coupe **80%**, 1600S engine **90%**, 1600 S90 engine **120%**
1960–1961 cabriolet **100%**, 1600S engine **150%**, 1600 S90 engine **180%**
1960–1961 Roadster **150%**, 1600S engine **170%**, 1600 S90 engine **200%**
1961–1962 Karmann Hardtop **50%**, 1600S engine **60%**
1962–1963 coupe **85%**, 1600S engine **100%**, 1600 S90 **140%**, four-cam **850%**
1962–1963 cabriolet **100%**, 1600S engine **150%**, 1600 S90 **240%**, four-cam **1800%**
1962 Roadster **200%**, 1600S engine **230%**, 1600 S90 engine **270%**

356C
1964–1965 coupe **95%**, SC engine **110%**, four-cam **700%**
1964–1965 cabriolet **110%**, SC engine **200%**

5 Before you view
– be well informed

The key to a successful purchase is research!
With over 75,000 examples produced over the 16-year production span, the variety of models and specification of the 356 and associated price considerations can make purchases daunting. Add to that the effects on value of poor and/or unauthentic restoration and there is really a lot to know. Before proceeding consult a dependable price guide and purchase an authenticity book.

Where is the car?
If your quest is for a specific model, be prepared to travel or hire an expert to do a pre-purchase inspection (PPI). It doesn't hurt to have a look at 356s for sale in your local area, even if not exactly the model on your wish list. Who knows? One may be the bargain of all time and alter your quest. On the other hand, if nothing else, you'll add to your knowledge base and refine the content of your enquiry list.

An original Porsche Kardex. Note lack of information.

Dealer or private sale?
Most dealers who handle 356s tend to be specialised in cars of this type and are apt to be at the top or above market prices. While any sort of warranty/guarantee is not likely, there is a good chance that they can hook you up with financing, which a private owner will not provide. Either source should be able to provide at least some history and have documentation, such as a Porsche Certificate of Authenticity (CoA).

The Porsche Certificate of Authenticity for the same car. What you didn't get: The two numbers on the top line are ignition key and door key codes. The dealer is Rossel & Co in Wiesbaden, which got a small warranty claim. The original owner's surname was Trepil.

PORSCHE

Certificate of Authenticity

The Porsche vehicle with identification number

10712

was manufactured with the following assembly specifications:

- Model Year/Type: 1951 356 Coupe
  Engine Number: 20252 506
  Transmission Number: Not Recorded
  Exterior Paint Color/Code: Radium Green P510
  Interior Material Color/Type: Green Leatherette

- Optional Equipment:
  None Recorded

PCNA 4172   5/14/97
Number   Porsche Cars North America, Inc.   Date

Cost of collection and delivery?

It is unlikely that you'll find a seller willing to deliver your new purchase halfway across the country, or even across town, for that matter. There are a number of carriers worldwide, though, that specialise in transport of classic cars. A phone call or email will provide you with a speedy quote. Alternatively, you can take a trailer, but it is wise to evaluate the car prior to arriving so equipped. It also aids in the bargaining phase not to appear too anxious.

When and where to view?

It is always preferable to view at the vendor's home or business premises. In the case of a private sale, the car's documentation should tally with the vendor's name and address. Arrange to view only in the daylight, and avoid a wet day. Most cars look better in poor light or when wet.

Reason for sale?

Make this one of the first questions. Why is the car being sold and how long has it been with the current owner? Are previous owners known? Consider contacting the previous owner to verify the details being given, if in doubt.

Left-hand to right-hand drive?

If a steering conversion has been done, it will certainly devalue any 356. They are best presented in the configuration as originally constructed, barring local road use regulations. Converted cars should be considered only keeping in mind the cost of reversing the changes.

Condition (body/chassis/interior/mechanicals)

Ask the seller for an honest appraisal of the car's condition. Ask specifically about some of the check items in chapters 7 and 9. Expect that the car will be somewhat less than in the condition described.

All original specification

Depending on your desires, this may or may not be important. Outlaw 356s can be worth more than the base model from which it is derived. Having said that, the vast majority of 356s will be worth much more if unmodified from original spec. Often you'll find the vendor has no idea. Take that authenticity book when you make your visit.

Matching data/legal ownership

Check that the VIN/chassis numbers and licence plate match the official registration document. Is the owner's name and correct address recorded in the official registration documents?

Ask who the car is insured with – seeing the owner's insurance certificate also helps confirm ownership, and the company may offer special deals for this type of car.

For countries that require tests for roadworthiness, does the car have one that is up to date? If appropriate, is the license plate current?

Does the vendor own the car outright? Several organisations will supply information based on the car's licence plate number for a fee. The information should indicate if your proposed purchase is stolen, recorded as having been

The stamped chassis number is here on cars built prior to 1962.

The secondary ID plate has additional information. Make sure it matches the stamped chassis number.

From 1962 onward everything is in the same place.

involved in an accident (in recent times only), has outstanding financing, or is being sought by the police or an insurance company.

Unleaded fuel

All but the very earliest 356s should run happily on unleaded fuel. There is more concern with fuel containing ethanol, which has corrosive effects on fuel lines, pump and carburettor parts. Ethanol-free fuel can be found in many locales, and generally is priced similarly to premium grade fuels and has comparable octane ratings.

Insurance

It is best to check with your current insurer, as well as with specialist insurers that cover classic cars, to determine what type of premium to expect. It is also wise to ascertain if your current insurer covers your test drive. If the vendor does not have a paid up policy, best to not press your luck.

How you can pay

Check with the seller about what is an acceptable method of payment. A cheque/ check will take several days to clear and the seller may prefer to sell to a cash buyer. However, a bankers draft (cashier's cheque/check issued by a bank) is as good as cash and much safer, just contact your bank for additional information. There is often a fee, but it is generally small.

Bank transfers are another way to complete the transaction without needing to carry uncomfortable amounts of cash.

Buying at auction?

If the intention is to buy at auction, see chapter 10 for further advice.

Professional vehicle check (mechanical examination)

Referred to in the US as a PPI (pre-purchase inspection), you will need to verify the expertise of inspector with 356 Porsches. Owner's clubs may be able to put you in touch with such marque/model specialists. An honest seller should not object to such an inspection. This type of inspection is quite helpful for long distance purchases. Spending several hundred dollars could very well save you the travel expense or even thousands for unexpected repair.

6 Inspection equipment
– these items will really help

Before you rush out the door, gather together a few items that will help as you work your way around the car.

Essential books
This book is designed to be your guide at every step, so take it along and use the check boxes in chapter 9 to help you assess each area of the car you're interested in.

Also take your authenticity book. Most sellers know their own car, but may be unaware of modifications made during the past 50 or 60 years. The wrong trim items could lead to a complete respray to put it right. Just because something is old, doesn't mean it is authentic. When in doubt, look it up.

Don't be afraid to let the seller see you using these books.

Reading glasses (if you need them for close work)
Take your reading glasses if you need them to read documents and make close-up inspections.

Magnet (not powerful, a flexible fridge magnet is ideal)
A magnet is used to detect unusual amounts of body filler or other non-ferrous corrosion or damage repairs. Be aware though, varying amounts of lead were used during the original assembly process and magnets don't stick to lead either.

Always ask the seller's permission about using a magnet, then if permission is granted, use it in appropriate places. Don't over use and by all means don't damage anything.

Torch (flashlight)
A torch with fresh batteries or recent charge will be useful for dark areas inside and below the car.

Probe (a small screwdriver works very well)
A small screwdriver can be used – with care – as a probe, particularly in areas on the underside of the car. With this you should be able to detect an area of severe corrosion, but be careful – if it is really bad, the screwdriver may penetrate the metal. The seller will not be amused if you poke several holes in his car.

Coveralls
Be prepared to get dirty. Take along a pair of coveralls, if you have them, and something dry to lie on when looking underneath the body. A chamois leather to dry the car if it is wet is also handy.

Mirror on a stick
Fixing a mirror at an angle on the end of a stick may seem odd, but you'll probably need it to check the condition of the underside of the car. It will also help you to peer into important crevices.

Digital camera
Your digital camera or phone is an important resource. It will allow you to remember all the things you forgot to look at. Take lots of pictures of everything at maximum resolution. Not only will they vastly improve your memory, but also will allow you to show areas of concern to others who may be more knowledgeable.

A sparkplug wrench and compression tester
To properly assess the functionality of the 356 engine, it is a good idea to check compression of all four cylinders. This is easy to do, though access to the front plugs can be a bit awkward on some models. If you are not familiar with 356s or the tool, bring along someone who is.

A fire extinguisher
These are mandatory at proper car shows. 356s that backfire or have float problems are known to occasionally light up one of the carburettors, which can lead to a disaster. A fire extinguisher can help prevent this. Also, know where the fuel valve in the interior is and how it works.

A friend, preferably a knowledgeable enthusiast
Ideally, have a friend or a knowledgeable enthusiast accompany you – a second opinion without rose tinted specs is always valuable.

Exterior

Unless informed otherwise, expect every 356 to have been totally or partially restored at least once at some point. Vast amounts of damage and repair may have been made dozens of years prior to the current caretaker's ownership. Don't expect them to know everything, unless they did the most recent one. If they did, ask if they can describe and show you pictures of what was done.

First take a quick walk around the car with doors and lids closed. Though it is hard to imagine, when the car originally left the factory, the gaps surrounding the moveable panels were absolutely uniform. The front and rear lids on the earliest cars had lead on the surrounding body panels, but shortly into production, tooling and assembly methods improved and lead was no longer needed.

Even door gaps indicate a well-preserved original car or a good quality restoration.

Doors, however, were fitted by measuring the bottom gap and cutting the front and rear ones. The front of each door and rear fender (and door jamb) have varying amounts of lead on all 356s. Lack of uniform gaps and/or flush fitting panels indicate less than perfect restoration.

1950 Reutter cabriolet in bare metal, showing areas of factory-applied lead.

Paint should be perfect and everything should match. There are no good ways to partially paint a 356, since there are no interruptions in the main body. With the exception of Speedsters, all 1950-1955 356 models were painted with nitrocellulose lacquer. Speedsters and all other 356s built from the 356A model forward used enamel paint. Modern basecoat clearcoat paints don't really resemble the subtle dimpling of enamel, but that is what you should expect. One last thing before moving on, 356s that don't have some paint chips on the nose are probably not actually driven.

Next check out the classic areas for body rust. On all cars this includes the rear of the front fenders, the front of the rear fenders, door bottoms and rocker panels. 356B and 356C cars also tend to rust above and below the headlights. Front and rear lids sometimes have penetrating rust in the skin above the hollow strengthening areas around the perimeter. If evidence of active rust or sloppy repair, start walking.

Run your hands around the insides of all four wheelarches. The exterior steel skin wraps around a wire to form the edge. It should feel like this and not vary in thickness. An exception to the uniform wire wrapped arch is the D'leteren Roadster. All four being the same is the desired outcome. Varying thickness is nearly always due to substandard body repairs.

Ask the seller if it is okay for you to open and close the lids and doors, or if he prefers to do this. If he wants to do it, this may be the reason why. Is the front lid kinked? Have a close look at the inner structure directly in front of the hinges. If it is cracked, looks funny or a patch is obvious, it is due to someone improperly closing the front lid, which on 1961 and earlier cars, may have happened when fuelling.

The wheelarch profile was originally constructed with the steel fender wrapped around a wire on nearly all 356s. Check all four for accident damage or sloppy repair.

A unique ratcheting mechanism in the lid hinges, front and rear, allow the lids to remain raised without a prop after opening and to close again only after raising them high enough to advance the ratcheting mechanism. Just pushing them down results in panel damage. You need to know this. If you are really good, you'll be able to make worn out hinges function using your index finger.

The inside of the front lid should be painted the colour of the car. Some 1956 and T 6 cars have a textured agent applied to the inside of the lid. Latch mechanisms on 1961 and earlier cars are also painted body colour. Luggage compartment walls and floor are black.

While up front, ask to have the spare tyre, jack and tool kit removed. No jack and tools? Make a note. Look also on the lid where it bolts to the left hinge. The last digit(s) of the chassis number should be stamped there. They are also on the doors (on the inner structure under the door panels) and rear lid. If there are no numbers, they are

The area where the battery sits should be nicely undercoated and free of rust. The coiled fog light wiring should be present when fog lights are not installed. Also note the vinyl side wall upholstery on this 1955 coupe.

replacement parts. If they are the wrong number(s), they started out on another car.

Now, look down where the battery is housed. The floor of this compartment in all likelihood has been replaced at least once. Look at it closely to determine if it was a quality job. It should look like it was always there and have nice, even rubberised undercoating (Body Schutz).

Next ask to have the rubber mat (plastic mat after 1961) removed. Look around

The chassis number is under the mat stamped into the floor of the luggage compartment above the battery area.

A second ID plate with the chassis number was located to the right of the fuel tank through 1961, and down by the stamped chassis number on later cars.

and find the stamped chassis number. It should match the one on the ownership documents and the one on a metal plate on the right side of the tank (in front of the tank after 1961). There's another one inside the driver's door, so let's go there next.

The number there is stamped on a silkscreened aluminium coachbuilder plate riveted on the aluminium panel that hides the door hinges. The plate may also include the exterior paint number. Does it match the exterior colour?

With the door completely open, run your fingers up and down inside the front fender through the door gap. You should only feel where the outer skin of the front fender uniformly wraps around the inner panel, not rust or evidence of casual rust repair.

Look also at the door jambs, striker plates and the condition of the threshold area. The bottoms of the doors, as well as the outer skins, are also subject to penetrating rust, so either use your mirror or lie down and take a good look – there should be shiny paint.

A third coachbuilder plate is riveted to the small aluminium panel that covers the left side door hinges. It also contains the stamped chassis number, and, on some cars, the paint number. On other cars a separate paint plate is below, which may or may not include the paint number.

The interior of the rear lid should be painted body colour, and the latch mechanisms on all 356s are also painted in this manner. The latch on the lid always has paint

Checking the area where the front fender sheet metal wraps around the inner structure for rust and/or poor quality repair.

The threshold area has a combination of rubber and aluminium trim. Door jamb area paint should seamlessly match the exterior body and have no signs of rust.

scratched off the mating surface. Make a note of the engine number while you are here.

356 coupes and cabriolets, and some 1956 356As, have vinyl upholstery surrounding the engine. It really is supposed to be there. All other models have black Body Schutz and a distinct-looking, tarpaper-like material called androplas, that assisted in sound deadening.

Now look underneath. Any penetrating rust means the car needs to be restored (or re-restored). To determine where to look for rust, have a look in parts catalogues from those who sell 356 restoration items. Any items they sell are what you should look at, including the floorpan, longitudinal members, and battery floor. Areas around the front and rear suspension are particularly critical.

Rubberised undercoat can cover up poor quality repairs. You should be able to see joints between all parts of the floorpan and chassis. The undercoating applied should be thin enough that the spot-welds holding everything together are visible. If things don't look right to you, have your expert verify that things look as they should. Anything wrong down here should eliminate this car as a viable purchase.

Interior

The 356 interiors are functional rather than showy. All models have painted dashboards. From early in the 1956 model year, and for all Speedsters, the paint matches the exterior colour. Earlier cars generally have a dark colour dashboard that coordinates well with the upholstery colour. If the exterior colour of the car is dark, it may be the same. Factory literature indicates that this tradition carried on through the beginning of 356A production, but I'm unaware of any actual examples. This is likely due to the fact that 356 model coupes and cabriolets had removable dashboards, making painting them a different colour uncomplicated.

The metal rails above the door panels and rear side interior panels on coupes and cabriolets match the dashboard through 1955, and coordinate with the interior colour on later cars, until they became upholstered from the introduction of the T 6 for the 1962 model year. Exceptions: the 'cheap' open cars – Speedster, Convertible D and Roadster – which were always upholstered and matched the door panels.

By now, you've probably asked for a copy of the official Porsche Certificate of Authenticity (CoA). Does the interior colour match? Is it leather and originally wasn't? Are the seats too plush and don't look like period factory photos? Oh, and does it have rubber floor mats, instead of carpet? Good, it should! The really cool ones are the tan mats used only in 356As.

German square weave carpet is correct for all but the very earliest cars. The edges are bound in cloth on coupes and cabriolets. Speedsters, Convertible Ds and some Roadsters were bound in vinyl. Binding generally matches the carpet colour, though some Speedsters with light-coloured carpet are bound in black. Karmann hardtops are very strange, with only the front pocket area and rear seatbacks bound in cloth.

Coupe headliners were a brushed cotton material through 1955, with later ones made from slightly off-white perforated vinyl. They should fit well and not be discoloured. Cabriolets have a full headliner, while other open cars do not. The inside surface of original German cloth tops is tan in colour and has a textured herringbone pattern.

Check to see that interior door handles and window cranks function and that plastic components, such as knobs, all match in colour and are not cracked.

The area behind and under the dashboard should be neat, with all wires and cables connected. Be sure to check that all electrical equipment and gauges function when the engine is running.

Under the dashboard should be neat and clean, with no stray electrical wires or components. The valve for the fuel tank should be set to AUF, and should show no sign of dripping gasoline.

Mechanicals

Ask the owner to remove the hubcaps. With these removed you should be able to see if the wheel date stamps match, and that they are all from a single manufacturer. It isn't a disaster if they aren't all the same, but an added bonus if they are. The visible part of the brake drums should be clean and dry. Brake rotors should be smooth and shiny. While you're there, how is the tyre wear?

Grab hold of the top of each front wheel and pull it toward you. It should not clunk. If it does, the front suspension might need to be rehabbed. Again, not a deal breaker, but it shows lack of attention. There should be minimal play in the steering. If there is, it may just need adjustment or maybe a steering box rebuild.

The clutch and brake pedals pivot from the floor, which many people find unusual. No 356 was originally fitted with a dual master cylinder, though many have been updated. Generally, this type of modification is considered acceptable due to the increased safety provided. Brake pedal feel should be firm with swift return and minimal travel. The clutch pedal should function in a similar fashion and pressure should not be excessive. Check also the handbrake function and make sure the fuel valve is set at Auf and is not dripping.

Look underneath the back of the car. Oil leaks from air-cooled engines are not surprising, but should not be excessive. Oil leaking where the gearbox bolts to the engine in all likelihood requires removal of the engine to address; maybe the gearbox, as well. Oil may also be leaking from the boots where the axles emerge from the gearbox. These are easily replaced, unless you want the type fitted when new, which are not held together with screws. Fluid leaks around any of the wheels are generally not good, and may influence your desire to have a test drive.

Next, fire up the engine and see how it idles. Only early

Technique for rocking the front wheels to assess condition of king and link pins.

cars have chokes, though some later ones have hand throttles to keep them from stalling when cold. When warm they should happily idle, unless the village mechanic has set it too low.

Make sure nothing is dripping, and that smoke does not continue to come from the exhaust. A little is normal at the very beginning. We all know, blue smoke – oil; black smoke – fuel; yes? Neither one is a good thing. During this time check the warning lights and gauges.

Check the engine number below the generator tower to see if it agrees with the CoA and other paperwork. Paint should not be overly shiny, and plating during the 356 era was silver (not gold) cad (cadmium). Carburettors generally have some fuel staining unless they are freshly rebuilt. Upholstering engine compartments ceased mid-1956.

Is it authentic?

This is really important, and can be difficult to determine. First, verify that all the information on the Porsche Certificate of Authenticity matches the car. Be aware that the information contained on the Certificate is not from the build record, but from the warranty card (Kardex). Many are sketchy or incomplete. Some are blank.

Use the authenticity book to verify things like lights, trim, instruments, body and chassis components. Many owners will not know that things are incorrect and are often agitated when they are pointed out. It is best to use discretion, but calculate the price of putting things right. Some things, like inappropriately installed or incorrect trim items, can result in a total respray.

To make the best use of your time, it is best to do your authenticity homework either before or immediately after your first encounter. Use the photos you took to help your memory. If you feel the necessity to buy the car before undertaking this step, you could end up spending thousands putting things right. This is also a major concern in an auction situation, when you don't get a rethink. Use the inspection time to do your due diligence.

Authenticity is very important when assessing value. This US-spec 1955 coupe has correct headlights, signal light lenses and bumper guards.

Restoration of a basket case

True or false? All the good basket cases have already been restored? You should assume that is true. Cost of a complete restoration will be at least ●50K for a fairly good car. Bad cars – plan to double or triple that, unless you do the majority of the work. Add that to the purchase price and you'll be upside down before you start – and once you start, if you don't finish, it will be worth less than what you paid for it.

Oh, and don't buy a 356 that is in boxes with or without restoration work being done. There are always parts missing, generally the things that are very expensive or impossible to find.

All 356s left the factory with impeccable fit and finish. Anything less diminishes the value considerably.

Any significant structural rust or body damage can turn many 356s into financial disasters.

Be wary of project cars with missing pieces.

A correct complete interior versus one needing work translates to thousands in your favourite currency.

A numbers-matching 356 with nice presentation is what you want to find.

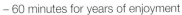

9 Serious evaluation
– 60 minutes for years of enjoyment

Score each section using the boxes as follows:
4 = excellent; 3 = good; 2 = fair; 1 = poor
The evaluation process utilising these numbers is described at the end of the chapter.

Exterior
Paint   4   3   2   1

First, evaluate the overall quality of the exterior paint. Is it a professional job without runs, dirt and other flaws? Are there chips, cracks or rust bubbles? Is the colour uniform on all panels? Does the colour match the information on the CoA? Is the paint surface period-correct? Older or flawed paintwork is not a deal killer, but it significantly affects the value of the car.

Other painted surfaces should be correct. Items that are body colour, should be and ones that were not, should not be. For example, the lid hinges should be painted correctly, body colour where they bolt to the lid and black where they attach to the body. The mounting hardware was also painted by hand after original installation. Chances are it won't be.

Other body colour items are described in Chapter 7.

Panel fit (gaps)   4   3   2   1
Gaps should be uniform and panel fit flush. The only exception is Gläser bodied cabriolets, where the leading edge of the doors is a little strange around the height of the top hinge.

Lids   4   3   2   1
The area in front of the hinge on the front lid should be perfect inside and out. The exterior skin was originally wrapped around the inner structural part and then spot-welded. The seam should be reasonably uniform and visible around the entire perimeter, and spot-weld dimples obvious inside the lids.

Shiny paint and perfect gaps equals show quality. Expect something less.

Doors   4   3   2   1
Doors have the same type wrap-around seam where the outer skin meets the inner structure. This cannot be seen at the front or rear, because it is lead-finished. It is visible along the bottom of the door, and should look like the seam on the lids, with no rust or separation. Hardware that secures the latch hardware and window frames, again,

Ugliness in front of the front lid hinges is a common finding. Repair in nearly all cases will include a total respray.

Door bottoms should be clean and rust-free. The outer skin wrap-around seam is only visible underneath.

was hand-painted after final assembly, but probably won't be. The heads of the mounting screws on the door jamb-mounted striker plates were also originally painted black.

Bumpers

Bumpers were originally fitted to the car so that the gaps to the body were even on the left and right, where they wrapped around the edges. This dimension was simplified at the rear from the introduction of the 356B, since they were bolted to the body at this time. Bumpers should also not droop at the ends.

Bumpers were nearly always painted body colour, though from 1956–1965 were very rarely chrome-plated. Bumpers were always steel.

Bumpers should fit nicely and not droop at the ends. Proper trim for model and year is important, as on this US-spec 1958 Speedster.

Proper fit and condition for convertible tops should be expected, as on this 356C cabriolet. The top frames can also be inspected on the lesser convertible models.

Soft top/ removable hardtop

Convertible top material was made by Happich and was referred to as All-wetter. A number of colours were used through 1955. All Speedsters and all 356As were available in black or tan. From the introduction of the 356B, grey was added. Regardless of colour, all tops had a tan herringbone pattern on the inside.

Tops should fit well with no wrinkles. The stitching on the seams should be intact, and the inside surface (headliner on cabriolets) should be devoid of stains and dirt. Rear windows were always plastic and should be in good condition. The top frame on non-cabriolet models should have paint that is not scratched or chipped.

Cabriolets have an aluminium tack strip above the rear window. On Reutter-built cabriolets through 1955, there is also one at the leading edge, as well as a body colour painted metal panel.

Removable hardtops for cabriolets were introduced for the 1958 model year. They had glass windows, and the rear seal had a bright aluminium insert. Fixed quarter windows were found only on 356As. Headliners were the same perforated vinyl used on coupes. Removable hardtops on cars with soft tops were optional,

Aftermarket fibreglass Speedster tops were a fairly common period accessory. Factory made ones were exceedingly rare.

though it was also optional to have one fitted without a soft top.

Fibreglass Speedster hardtops were made by a variety of aftermarket companies in the US, and Porsche apparently made a few metal ones. The latter would probably command a premium, but the fibreglass ones usually don't.

All cabriolets originally came with top boots, except 1958 and later cars

From 1958 through 1965, cabriolets could be fitted with hard tops. Either or both tops could have been ordered. (Courtesy Dave Derossett)

ordered with only the hardtop. German-style Tenax studs were present on the body for mounting them. Cabriolet boots were made from the same cloth used for the tops. Speedsters featured a vinyl half tonneau rather than a boot, and optional vinyl boots were offered on Convertible D and Roadsters.

Optional full tonneaus in upholstery quality vinyl were available for all open cars, though first use is unknown. From 1958, cabriolet tonneaus were made from the same cloth used for tops. The only time optional items are expected is when they are listed on the CoA.

Rust areas

Rust areas on the body and chassis were mentioned in Chapter 7. Add to the list the fender braces. Cars with no other damage will potentially have rust in the battery area, due to the presence of the battery and its corrosive contents.

Perhaps worse than the rust itself is poor quality repair, and covering this up in an attempt to deceive buyers. In most cases this can be discovered by thoroughly examining the problem areas from both sides, where possible. Your magnet may help here, but your eyes and hands are key to determining actual condition.

If you find any significant rust or any poor quality repair, you really don't need to total up the points; just go home and find another car.

4 3 2 1

Battery compartment rust is common, even if no rust is present elsewhere. This 356A coupe has the added benefit of having a nose- full of pink polyester body filler.

Unusual contours around the rear of the front fender and non-uniform thickness of the fender arch are signs that you should find another car.

Crash areas ☐4 ☐3 ☐2 ☐1

These are primarily front and rear dead centre. It is not easy to observe the inner surface of the nose or tail due to the way they are concealed by the inner structural panels. Again, with eyes and hands, try to assess the condition. Phone cameras are also useful. Holes with plastic body filler emerging like polyester worms from the inside of external nose or tail panels are another indication of a really bad repair.

Body damage tends to be centre front or centre rear. An honest car that has not been repaired is a blessing. Lots of other issues on this 356B coupe include door and fender rust, along with a droopy rear bumper end.

Exterior trim ☐4 ☐3 ☐2 ☐1

Not a deal breaker, but potentially expensive is the replacement or repair of exterior trim. In this area, replacement of exterior trim with incorrect parts or inferior reproduction items is the main problem. If you don't know the difference, potentially you're in trouble. Most reproduction items are pretty good now, but reproductions began less than ten years after production stopped. There have been over a dozen different bumper guard reproductions for 356 and 356A cars. They may look just fine, but they don't look anything like the originals.

Early exterior mirror reproductions had significant flaws and these were gradually improved over time – one at a time. Mirrors also should not be

Missing or damaged exterior trim should alert you to future expenses. This 356A coupe is expressing this and more besides.

mounted on the doors unless a mirror access hole is in the front of the door – introduced March 1957.

How about the colour of the orangey-red enamel on the Porsche hood crest? For years, the official Porsche-supplied version looked nothing like the original. Copyright violating reproductions were vastly superior: well, more authentic at least.

Good quality chrome plating these days is very expensive, and often it is more cost-effective to replace original items that need to be plated. The good news is that there is not that much chrome-plated trim on a 356. There is also not a great deal of anodized aluminium trim prior to the T 6 356B, and even then, not so much. Most of these items can be purchased as good quality reproductions.

Rubber seals ☐4 ☐3 ☐2 ☐1

While all rubber seals are available either as OEM or reproduction parts, they don't all fit or survive the same. Consult the clubs for opinions about which to use, if needed. Though not particularly expensive, having to replace just about anything is labour intensive and kind of a pain; some things more so than others.

While this side window seal is available and inexpensive, having to partially dismantle the door to replace it more than makes up for the affordability.

Wipers

Inserts are easy; authentic blades and arms less so, some substantially less so. Manufacturer's marks should be visible on blades.

Lights

Reproduction lights have been available for years. Many do not have the German K number codes or appropriate manufacturer's marks. While specialists can provide this service, it is expensive, and with manufacturer's marks, not technically legal. Always check lights and lenses very carefully. Some OEM ones had no markings, especially on older models. Other later or recent production OEM lenses and light units are modified from original specification – some substantially.

Headlights are a particular problem. There are a number of different options out there, and the reproduction units that have been available for decades were all made for the VW Beetle market. Consult your authenticity book to determine the correct lights for your car. Sealed beam units with a little parking light bulb in the front were only used for two years on 356s. Recently, some new more correct sealed beam lenses have become available.

Until recently, glass reflectors for 356 and 356A models with K numbers were not available, and originals were quite difficult to find. Many cars have the later ones made by ULO.

Window trim and glass

Laminated glass was used for all windshields, back glass on very early coupes and pop-out rear quarter windows. All laminated glass was originally made by Sigla.

Tempered glass was used for side windows and later rear glass. These were made by Sekurit.

Original glass logos (bugs) should be present on all glass. This is a laminated coupe quarter window made by Sigla.

All glass should have the manufacturer logo etched into the surface. Newer replacement windshields have more and more information required by law, which looks decidedly non-original. It is reported that cars with non-OEM replacements do not lose points at car shows. If that's what you are planning to do, assume this is incorrect.

There are currently replacements for most other non-windshield glass, but some of it is really pricey. If chips or scratches on your original glass concern you, do some research.

Replacing windshields on Speedsters, Convertible Ds and Roadsters is not recommended for the squeamish. Will the glass shop guarantee they won't break it when installing?

All 356s had five-lug wheels. Through the end of drum brake use they had a wide pattern, similar to period VWs. The disc brake wheels on 356Cs had a smaller five-lug arrangement.

The earliest 356s had solid wheels that were used on contemporary VWs sized 16 x 3in. Mid-year 1951 slotted wheels were introduced and used through the end of the 1955 model year. They were also 16in diameter and 3.25in wide.

Original wheels on pushrod 356s built from 1956–1965 were 15in diameter and were not wider than 4.5in – ever. Wider disc brake wheels were manufactured, but these were always for 911/912. The 5.5in wide drum brake chrome-plated wheels are not authentic, and probably made in Brazil. The chrome plating isn't really very good quality either.

For 356s not everything is black and white. You may appreciate modern disc brakes on a Speedster, but if I am buying the car, the original brake drums and wheels had better be included in the purchase price.

For that matter, factory chrome-plated wheels were not very common either. If the CoA doesn't call them out, assume they are wrong. Silver painted wheels will make the car stand out at every show, regardless. Earlier cars with other colour wheels and/or pinstriping, are just more distinctive.

All four wheels should be of the same manufacturer and have similar, if not identical, date stamps. Tyres are up to you. Period sizes and brands are my favourites.

Hubcaps are a problem with early cars, because so many VW moons are out there. Original hubcaps are pointier, but positive identification is difficult. Price is important, though.

T 2 356As are the first to have the ones with the enamelled Porsche crest. Disc brake wheel hubcaps at first had no centre crests, then the enamelled ones, then ones with no enamel.

Interior
Seats   4   3   2   1
Seats used in the earliest coupes and cabriolets were substantial, and did not recline. In general, coupes used cloth material, and cabriolets, leather. For the most part, leather is found on subsequent cabriolet front seats, with cloth, vinyl and optional leather for coupes. In cabriolets, other panels were usually vinyl with similar colour and leather grain pattern. Full leather was an unusual option (much more common on restored cars) on all models.

Up to 1953, reclining seats were offered, sometimes on just one seat. These are generally Keiper recliners made in Germany, though other aftermarket sources also made them. The 1953 Super models in the US all came with recliners made by Recaro. These were no doubt the sole option for cars sold in the rest of the world.

A bench seat option was available as early as 1952, but were rarely fitted. The later ones had the same Recaro recliners on the individual driver and passenger

Replacement of seats and other missing or severely damaged interior items on a project car can add up to significant amounts. Aluminium patch panels on the floor are also a bad thing.

seatback. Recliner evolution can be found in your authenticity book. Check to make sure that recliners function and fore and aft seat adjustment can be made.

Seat backs became a lot less sofa-like at the T 2 model break in 1958 and remained so until the end of 356C production. Other changes were seat rail changes in 1962 and the addition of locks to prevent accidental folding function in 1964.

A special lightweight seat was made for the Speedster, though regular reclining seats could be ordered as optional equipment. The Speedster seat had a pressed steel bucket and had thin padding. It did not recline, but tipped forward on hinges mounted to a wooden frame and used the same seat rails as other models. Later GT cars had aluminium shells for weight saving. Most were finished in vinyl and often had contrasting piping. On most '55 models the piping matched the exterior colour. The seatback was carpeted.

Convertible Ds had normal reclining seats, but Roadsters came standard with a boomerang-shaped non-reclining hinge.

Upholstery has nearly always been replaced at least once on any 356. Because of this, finding something that looks original means knowing what that looked like, which is the hard part. Many times the colours or padding are not correct, and that means the only remedy is another replacement. On the other hand, if you don't mind the non-authentic part of it, you might still want to mention it during price negotiations.

Rear seats in the earliest coupes and cabriolets went through an evolution from lumps in the carpet to an actual seat cushion with folding seatback. Material matched the front with the vinyl most often replacing leather as mentioned above. At the 356B model change, each rear seat had small individual cushion and folding seatback.

Exceptions: Speedsters had cushions, but rarely seatbacks. Convertible D and Roadsters have only carpet, though there was a rarely fitted optional seat cushion available on Roadsters. Karmann Hardtop models have individual rear seat cushions and backs with unique carpeting and upholstery.

Carpet

⟨4⟩ ⟨3⟩ ⟨2⟩ ⟨1⟩

With the exception of the first 356s in 1950/51, all carpet was German square weave, which came in a variety of colour choices. The colour is rarely listed on the CoA, but is generally associated with upholstery colours. Carpet colours were not the same for every year. Consult your authenticity book for details.

If the carpet shows anything but minimal wear or is not correct, a number of suppliers provide complete sets. The price is in Chapter 2 and does not include installation.

Floor mats

⟨4⟩ ⟨3⟩ ⟨2⟩ ⟨1⟩

All 356s have wooden floorboards in the pedal area. 1955 and earlier cars also have wooden false floors for clutch cable clearance. Covering them is a floor mat made of rubber. There are also separate rear mats, and a mat covering the front

356s built prior to the 1956 model year had not only front floorboards, but also false floors made of wood. This makes the centre tunnel nearly flush. Note also the contrasting colour of the dashboard.

centre tunnel area around the shift lever and heat controls. The back half of the tunnel is carpeted.

The material used on the earliest cars was a fine ribbed industrial looking rubber that was cut to fit. Shortly into production, certainly by the 1952 model year, moulded black rubber mats replaced the earlier style.

Starting with the 356A, the tunnel mat went from being ribbed texture to pebble grain. 356B and 356C models were also pebble grained.

All remaining mats were moulded and had a ribbed pattern with pebble grain edges. They are generally black, but some T 2 356As with tan or oatmeal carpets have tan ones.

Most of these mats are available as quality reproductions. Many choose to cover the ones up front with Coco (also cocoa/koko) mats to make the interior look less utilitarian. They were offered as factory accessories from 1956, perhaps earlier. There are multiple suppliers; originals faded rapidly and were not rubber backed.

Headliner

Headliner material is described in Chapter 7. Condition is everything and, again, most will have been replaced in the past. The early soft cloth type was especially prone to stains from water. The desirable sliding steel sunroof option that began in 1954 was apparently not particularly watertight.

The material used for the perforated vinyl headliners in 356A – and later coupes, removable hardtops and Karmann hardtops – had a diamond pattern to the holes, which were pierced. Many replacement headliners used a material that has a square pattern with punched holes. These later vinyl headliners were also subject to staining and deterioration. Be aware that replacement requires removing front and rear glass, as well as the rear quarter windows. Before reinstallation, rubber seals should also be replaced.

The cloth headliners in cabriolets also stain and deteriorate with use. Replacement of these, as well as the other types mentioned above, should be done by a competent auto upholstery shop.

Sun visors fitted to the cars through

White perforated vinyl headliners tended not to age well, with wrinkles and discolouration not to mention larger perforations. Proper materials were not always available. Replacement means removal of all the glass, which can create other problems.

1955 were dark-coloured plastic with chrome-plated frames. All other cars had padded vinyl visors, which did not pivot to the side. The latter may have been fitted with vanity mirrors on the passenger's side. Speedsters did not have visors; they were optional on Convertible Ds, and Roadsters came standard with one, and the passenger's side was optional. Plastic and vinyl do not age well, but reproductions are available.

A confusing array of interior mirrors were fitted through the years, and some have been reproduced. Again, it is important to know whether the correct one is fitted, and not just evaluate condition.

Original upholstery is generally not a plus.

Other upholstery

Door panels, rear side panels and the firewall panels on coupes nearly always match the colour and texture used on the seats. On open cars, door panels and panels behind the doors (when present) also match the seat colour and texture. If the seats are leather, the other upholstery panels can be leather also, but few cars were originally so equipped. The card stock that backed these panels warps with age and water damage. All are replaceable at a cost.

With the exception of Speedsters and some 1953 models, door panels incorporated a full-length pleated pocket at the bottom of the doors. They are generally vinyl or leather, even if the door panels are cloth-covered. Since Convertible Ds and Roadsters did not have glove boxes, the driver's side panel, and occasionally the passenger's as well, incorporated a locking pocket.

A strange tan textured vinyl was used initially on 1955 models, and occasionally in later years, called acella bast (basket-weave). It was most commonly found on Speedsters, but made its way to other models on rare occasions. My personal opinion is that most cars originally equipped lost it, not due to damage, but because people didn't think it was factory installed.

Interior trim

The dashboard paint on early cars was described in Chapter 7. The 1950-1951 interior door top, and above the rear side panels in coupes, were wood and often tinted with the colour of the dashboard. The door tops on Reutter cars incorporated a finger grip on top to help passengers close the doors. These were not found on Gläser cabriolets.

From 1953, these were steel on coupes and cabriolets, and were painted to match the dashboard and complement the interior colour: only very rarely were they the exterior colour of the car. On cabriolets, the inside of the windshield frame was painted this

1951 Gläser cabriolet with rare matching dashboard paint. Also present are tinted wood door tops and velour carpet with contrasting red binding. The Petri steering wheel was also a period accessory for VW beetles.

colour as well. Also, the leading edge of the steel dash top from 1956 was painted to coordinate with the colour of the dash top pad.

Speaking of 1956, the one-year-only colour chart lists coupes and cabriolets with dashboards not matching exterior colour. It is uncertain if any such cars were produced.

Chrome-plated interior door pulls were used from 1952 through T 6 356Bs on all models except Speedsters. 356Cs had armrests with finger grips. Earlier optional armrests 1959–1963 did not have finger grips.

The earliest door handles and window cranks had plastic escutcheons, which were the ones used on period deluxe VW beetles. All plastic parts were an ivory colour and were used through the 1953 model year.

In 1954, Porsche incorporated their own knobs onto the VW window cranks and added their own escutcheons. They came in three colours: tan, grey and ivory. They matched the dashboard knobs and steering wheel colour through the end of the 356A model. The actual cranks and door handles changed to a newer VW versions at the T 2 model change and the escutcheons were smaller diameter. As a rule of thumb: tan plastics were used with red upholstery; ivory with tan or brown; grey with grey or black.

A small number of very late 356As had black plastic components as did all remaining 356Bs and 356Cs.

Steering wheel   [4] [3] [2] [1]

Steering wheels on the first 356s were produced by Petri in two diameters, 400mm and 425mm, and an optional Pealit model featured a horn ring. All were ivory in colour, with plain ivory centre horn buttons.

The two spoke VDM wheel was introduced with the 1953 models and included the first appearance of the Max Hoffman-inspired Porsche crest horn button. This wheel was produced in the same two diameters as the earlier wheel, and when fitted with a horn ring the central button flashed the headlights on 356As.

The first VDM wheels were ivory in colour, but grey and beige were added in 1954 to match the dashboard and door mounted plastics. It is worth noting that these and earlier wheels were painted plastic, which makes them relatively easy to restore.

The final standard wheel was also made by VDM and fitted to all 356Bs and 356Cs. It had a black painted plastic rim, was slightly dished, had three spokes and could be fitted with an optional horn ring. Many have been converted to wood rims, since this service is offered and owners often perceive wood rimmed wheels to make the car more desirable.

Wood steering wheels were optional from 1956 on, possibly earlier. Factory supplied ones were made by VDM and Nardi. Most are available

Large 425 mm diameter beige VDM steering wheel without horn ring. Horn functioned via the centre button, which flashed headlights on cars equipped with horn rings. Note also Speedster seats with red contrasting piping.

The later VDM steering wheel used for 356B and 356C models is somewhat more difficult to restore.

as reproductions. Good ones are pricey and originals much more so. Period aftermarket wheels made by Nardi and Derrington can command some fairly high prices, as well.

Modern aftermarket wheels, including leather ones, diminish the value of the car. Reproduction wood wheels add no real value and are a matter of personal preference unless called out in the CoA.

Instruments

As with many of the items on 356s, replacement of instruments was often a quick fix for a non-functional gauge. The date stamps are located on the back of the instruments, so a basic knowledge component is necessary. The chronological changes and variations based on engine originally fitted are beyond simple memorization. Further complicating this is the fact that the large instrument diameters stayed the same throughout the entire production from 1950–1965 making it possible to fit any instrument in any 356. Consult your authenticity book.

The condition and functionality of instruments is important, but all can be rebuilt at reasonable prices. Rims, faces and indicators can be replaced in most cases with correct ones for the car even if substitute gauges are present. Having said that, incorrect instruments should be considered a reflection of attention to detail.

Some of the older instruments, such as the pneumatic fuel gauge and capillary oil temperature gauges used prior to 1956, can be challenging to replace or repair. Even the oldest clocks, on the other hand, should be operable or repairable.

Dashboard switchgear

Switches for headlights, wipers, turn signals and such should be functional and correct with appropriate matching knobs. As with instruments, these were frequently replaced with whatever was handy at the time the original part failed. In most cases, replacements are only available as used parts and unlike instruments, they are difficult to put right if they have rusty parts or are not functional. Replacement knobs are no problem.

Many times, switches have been put where they didn't belong, and this requires welding up holes and repainting the dashboard. Again, it is important to know how things are supposed to look and where switches should be mounted. Is anything missing?

While it might seem an insignificant area, problems here are difficult and potentially expensive to correct.

Handbrake and pedals

Handbrake mechanisms should be complete and functional. While there were different permutations over the years, it is highly improbable one was replaced with the wrong type. There should be plenty available used and, since demand is low, they should be cheap.

All of these are cable-operated, and should hold the car on a grade. If it doesn't, they probably just need adjustment, a minor consideration.

All three pedals on all 356s hinge from the floor, unlike many cars. While this may take some getting used to, a bigger concern is that the location makes them subject to damage by corrosion. They are bolted to the sheet metal floorpan, and if that is really rusted badly, they are bolted to nothing.

Corrosion can also occur in the pedal mechanism bushings or hinge on the accelerator pedal. These can all be remedied at minimal cost, but if any pedal sticks or doesn't return properly, your test drive might be more of an adventure than expected.

Front compartment

Clean and neat

This is a pretty stark area, but the presence of the battery often led to rust problems, even in climates where other areas were not so affected. A nice, neat battery floor probably has been replaced, but if done well, should not give a clue. There should be no obvious welded patches, or indeed, any trace of gas welding, since only spot welds were utilised during original construction. It should be covered with an even coat of black rubberised Body Schutz, as should all sidewall surfaces.

The steering box access cover is found under the mats described below. Paint may be satin black or Body Schutz. The surrounding area on 356 and 356As is covered with Body Schutz. On T 5 356Bs it is textured androplas. T 6 356 Bs and 356Cs have fuel tanks in this area, and the surface surrounding them should be Body Schutz.

Sidewalls on cars built prior to 1956, and possibly some 1956 models, were upholstered. Through 1954 they were carpet bound in cloth. Later cars had a textured vinyl, which usually matched the engine compartment upholstery. Speedsters didn't have upholstery.

Minimal luggage space in earlier cars is further compromised by the presence of factory-supplied tool and travel kits. Speedsters had cloth tyre straps, while other models had leather. (Courtesy Steve Douglas)

Fuel tank

While there was an evolution of fuel tanks from 1950–1961, all of them share the same location, the same satin black finish, and the same large fuel cap manufactured by Blau with a finely ribbed edge. Check your authenticity book if you are unsure whether the tank is correct.

Fuel level senders were first incorporated during the 1954 model year. Speedsters didn't get them until the 356A model break. Along with early cars with no fuel gauge, they were equipped with a calibrated wooden stick to assess fuel level.

External fuel fillers were first incorporated at the introduction of the T 6 body style, though it was delayed on RHD cars, possibly as late as April 1964. The first external filler fuel tanks had the sender on the bottom of the tank, which was replaced mid-1962 by one with the sender on top. The earlier tanks were

The optional 80-litre tank, available through 1961, left no room for luggage.

black; the later ones light grey. Both were topped with androplas in the centre. Cars with the later tanks are less prone to sender and leakage problems.

The standard 356A and T 5 356B fuel tank capacity was 57 litres, though an optional 80-litre tank was offered as early as 1956. The standard T 6 tank was 52 litres, with an optional 70-litre tank offered on all models. The latter was on all Carrera 2s not fitted with the even larger 110-litre version. Large tanks are a desirable addition, though they significantly limit luggage capacity.

Mat

The earliest cars came equipped with mats made of the same industrial fine-ribbed rubber mats used on the interior floor. Some cars were carpeted. In 1953, when the tyre placement was more vertical a black moulded rubber mat was between the tyre and the tank. T 6 cars have a moulded black ABS plastic mat embossed with the word PORSCHE in extended letters. This mat is modified for cars with larger tanks.

RHD T 6 tanks and earlier cars with oversize fuel tanks have no mats. Quality versions of both types of mat are available for a reasonable price.

Chassis number(s)

The chassis number should be stamped into the structural inner chassis toward the front of the luggage compartment. On cars through the T 5 356B another aluminium plate was located on the luggage compartment floor to the right of the fuel tank. On later cars these were directly to the right of the stamped number.

Obviously, the numbers on the two should match. The aluminium plate will also contain additional information, which should match the information on the CoA.

In the early days, cars that were damaged beyond repair were often rebuilt by Reutter using an exchange chassis. These often have the original number with a line through it and the replacement number stamped in the chassis. There were three series of these from 1953–1965 and one series duplicated some of the numbers used on 1952 Gläser-bodied cabriolets (oops!).

Stolen cars have been known to have numbers that were either beyond the end point of actual production or number combinations never used by Porsche. The

The 70-litre T 6 tank left little space for luggage up front. (Courtesy Charles Coker)

Up front in the 356C: ABS plastic floor mat, tool kit, plastic washer tank and fuse block cover.

Location of stamped chassis number, and aluminium manufacturer plate on the T 6 356.

current owner may not have any idea. It is probably polite to inform them, before you walk away.

Spare wheel, jack and tools ④ ③ ② ①

Spare wheels should have the same date code as other wheels and be the same manufacturer, size and configuration. There were no space saver spares in this era.

All jacks were supplied by Bilstein. The earlier VIGOT type had a screw lift mechanism with a ratcheting handle. The later one was smaller diameter and worked via a pump action. They were similar to the ones found in period VWs. 356 ones have an angled peg, rubber buffer at the top and generally have a light blue base. While people actually used these long ago, don't even think about it. Carry a small scissors or floor jack, better yet a classic car insurance card.

Tool kits are too difficult to describe here. Consult your authenticity book. Like the jack, these tools are something else you will never use. They are important for high level shows and personal satisfaction. They almost never survived intact. Replica kits are out there, but tend to be pricey. The round tin kit that fits in the centre of the spare wheel is a VW accessory.

Electrical items,
washer system and heater/blower ④ ③ ② ①

The fuse panel on 1962 and later cars is mounted to the left-side back wall (earlier cars have them under the dashboard). Covers on 356B ones are fibreboard, 356C white plastic.

Disc brake wheel date stamp showing August 1963. (Courtesy Larry Haskett)

Early VIGOT Bilstein jack, slatted wood floor and glass SWF washer bottle are characteristic of very early cars. Note also the wood fuel dipstick for this car that is not fitted with a fuel gauge.

The washer bottle on all T 6 cars is mounted on the other side. Both were held in place with black rubber bands with metal hooks.

The earliest cars had glass washer bottles held in place by a steel cage and were manufactured by SWF. In the first cars they were down by the battery with some later cars up by the fuel tank. The 1955 model had a vinyl bag on the left side of the fuel tank and stayed that way through the end of T 5 production.

All 356 washers were operated by a hand pump mounted under the dashboard. The 356A had a foot pump left of the clutch, with later cars having a rubber foot pump. Electrically operated washers were available from 1962.

The first 356s had slatted wooden platforms below the uncovered battery located to the right. When the spare tyre arrangement changed for the 1953 model, the battery became centrally located and sat on a small black wooden platform. Platforms were discontinued in mid-year 1956, and the Speedster had a smaller one, presumably meaning they had a smaller battery(?).

From 1953 the battery was also covered. The first covers were steel and were held down with spring latches. These are potential fire hazards and should either not be used or at least verify that the positive battery terminal is well covered. Fibreboard covers replaced these in mid-1956 and with minor modifications remained in used through the T 5 356B. At this point the battery was again moved to a right of centre location. These initially had fibreboard covers, which were replaced early on by black ABS ones.

Alongside the T 6 battery there was room to accommodate a fresh air blower or Eberspächer gasoline heater. Both are fairly rare. It is a plus if they work.

Engine compartment
Clean and neat

There will generally be some fuel staining on the carburettors and manifolds. Inline fuel filters are often fitted, though not authentic. Presence of some oil contamination is not unusual, though freshly rebuilt engines should be clean.

Metal shrouds should be nicely painted with satin finish. All are black through 1957. The main fan shroud on Supers, Super 90s and SCs are lighter colours. The progression was silver to an off-white.

Correct engine

The engine number should match the one on the CoA, if the car is being presented as matching numbers. Though highly unethical, changing the engine number to match has certainly been done.

If the engine is not the original one, you need to decide how important that is. It does have an effect on the value. Having said that, many changes were indiscriminately done in the era when 356s were just used cars. This may make you question an iffy car with matching engine. If concerned, take photos and consult an expert.

Correct carburettors/
fuel system

Upgrades in carburettors should be taken for what they are. If performance is important to you, maybe a sub-100 horsepower 356 isn't your cup of tea. Original carburettors and air filters are what is expected. All original type carburettors can be rebuilt by experts and made to run like new.

Decision time with a 1600 Normal-powered 356A T 2 Speedster. Do you want to go fast with incorrect carbs and paint your fan shroud the wrong colour?

Wiring and
ignition system

Visible wiring should have proper fittings and no splices. Original distributors and not performance VW ones are desired. Plug wires were originally black, but expect them to be something else. Blue coils hadn't been invented in 1965, but all of this stuff is inexpensive to rectify.

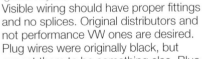

Or – do you want the engine to look like a 1600 Normal? (Courtesy Fred Harper)

Side and rear walls

Vinyl upholstery is found in all non-Speedsters until early 1956. From that point, sprayed Body Schutz is present on sides and rear. The firewall had a jute pad to aid in sound deadening.

The voltage regulator was also above and to the right of the engine. All were made by Bosch. The rectangular black ones are correct from 1955 through the end of the T 6 356B model. Earlier cars had them on top of the generator. There were a number of varieties that evolved over time. The 356C had a smaller square one with an aluminium housing. None of these are available new at this time.

Mechanical

Engine

At this point, if allowed, this is a good time to check cylinder compression. All readings should be consistent. Low readings for one or more means at least a valve job; maybe a total engine rebuild. Cylinders at the flywheel end tend to be a little lower.

Oil leaks were mentioned in Chapter 7. Leaks at the crankshaft seals at either end mean engine removal for repair.

A little oil smoke when first starting the engine is normal with air-cooled engines. Ask your expert about any odd noises or have it checked by a competent mechanic.

Clutch

When running, depress the clutch pedal. If you hear a whine, it usually means the throw out bearing will need replacing. If it engages very high or very low, it probably just needs to be adjusted.

Gearbox

Leaking gearbox oil from anywhere is not to be expected. Unrestored vehicles tend to have gearboxes covered with dirt and grease, making it difficult to identify drips. If leaking from the bell housing, this generally indicates a leaking pinion seal, which requires at least engine removal.

You should also be able to engage all gears while parked.

Brakes

Make sure that there is brake pressure. If there is significant pedal travel and the handbrake also doesn't work, skip the test drive and ask the owner to have it fixed, if you are still interested in test driving the car.

Dual-function master cylinders were not original equipment, but the car may be updated. It is your decision if authenticity is important in this critical area. The aluminium reservoirs fitted to early cars are also prone to bi-metallic corrosion and subsequent leaks. Plastic ones are safer and may have been fitted.

Front suspension and steering
The simple checks for this area are described in Chapter 7.

Dampers (shock absorbers)
These should be checked for leaks. You can also check function by pushing down on the fender a couple of time to see if it continues to bounce after stopping.

Replacements are cheap and easily replaced. The rear lever shocks on very early cars can be rebuilt by specialists.

Wiring

All of the visible wiring should be clean and neat. There are a few extra wires in some models (such as those up front for fog/driving lights), but there shouldn't be a rat's nest of dirty, twisted, spliced and loose wires. A replacement wiring harness costs around ●2000, not including installation.

If you haven't already, check to see if everything electrical works.

Battery

Make the effort to look at the battery. This means removing the spare wheel and battery cover. Check for corroded terminals and condition of the floor in this area. Ground straps should be flat woven copper. It is best to have the positive terminal covered, though originally they weren't.

If there is no battery cover, all are available as reproductions, except the early metal ones.

Under the dashboard should be well manicured. Early pre-transistor cars have a braided cable going from the radio to under the passenger side floorboard, where the amplifier box is located.

Exhaust and heat exchangers

These are available, though not inexpensive. There is no repair other than replacement. Non-original exhaust systems are frequently fitted. They tend to be loud and offer minimal performance enhancement. Do some research, so that you know what is correct and what replacements cost.

Test drive

Does the starter have any trouble turning over the engine? Most 356s are 6-volt, and starters generally perform at a leisurely pace. The engine should come to life with minimal cranking and idle happily when warm.

If everything seems okay, go for a drive. It doesn't need to be really long,

Very clean underbody with no obvious oil leaks and pristine exhaust system. Tail pipe extensions are a useful accessory that keep rear bumper guards free from exhaust contamination.

but you need to be able to sample all of the gears. As stated before, earlier 356s like to be shifted gently, with those from 1959 being less fussy. Any crunch is a potential bad thing, especially going from first to second. All cars from the 1953 model year have syncros on all forward gears, so downshifting should also be crunch-less. Don't be too enthusiastic going down into first, as a general precaution.

The gearbox throws on pre-1960 cars are long and imprecise feeling. On later cars they are shorter but still feel vague due to the somewhat primitive linkage.

You should expect to hear some gear noise in first and second gear, but it should be minimal in third and fourth. The exhaust note and wind noise will also be prominent sounds.

To assess clutch function, try starting off in third gear. The engine should die. If it revs freely or slips in other gears while being driven, the clutch needs to be replaced. These are not particularly expensive.

When you stop, does it pull to one side? This can be due to structural damage or something as simple as wheel cylinders that are not adjusted correctly or installed backwards on one of the front wheels. Only one of these is easy to fix.

Steering effort should be low and the car shouldn't wander. Any play in the steering should be suspect. If it feels like the rear end is about to spin out at low speeds, check the tyre pressure. It is probably low in the rear.

Just for fun, open the floor-mounted vents and turn the heater knob (or pull the knob/lever) all the way on. Does rust blow out the vents and defroster? How about heated air?

Evaluation procedure

Add up the points scored.

160 to 180 = show to near show quality. Will you be afraid to drive it?

136 to 159 = good to very good driver quality. Price should reflect areas needing attention.

115 to 135 = depends on where the low marks are found. Can you live with it as is or afford to fix the problems?

91 to 114 = ditto above. Give your calculator a good workout.

90 and below = a pricey project. You probably can't afford the risk.

Is it worth the price?

Use a current price guide such as the one found at www.hagerty.com to assess the overall condition and asking price. Don't be afraid to offer what you consider to be the appropriate number. Always leave your contact information, even if your offer is turned down.

10 Auctions
– sold! Another way to buy your dream

Auction pros & cons
Pros: Prices are usually lower than those of dealers or private sellers, and you might grab a real bargain on the day. Auctioneers have often established clear title with the seller. At the venue you can examine documentation relating to the vehicle.
Cons: You have to rely on a sketchy catalogue description of condition and history. The opportunity to inspect is limited and you cannot drive the car. Auction cars are often a little below par and may require some work. It's easy to overbid. There may be a buyer's premium to pay in addition to the auction hammer price.

Which auction?
Auctions by established auctioneers are advertised in car magazines and on the auction houses' websites. A catalogue, or a simple printed list of the lots for auctions might only be available a day or two ahead, though often lots are listed and pictured on auctioneers' websites much earlier. Contact the auction company to ask if previous auction selling prices are available as this is useful information (details of past sales are often available on websites).

Catalogue, entry fee and payment details
When you purchase the catalogue of the vehicles in the auction, it often acts as a ticket allowing two people to attend the viewing days and the auction. Catalogue details tend to be comparatively brief, but will include information such as 'one owner from new, low mileage, full service history,' etc. It will also usually show a guide price to give you some idea of what to expect to pay and will tell you what is charged as a 'Buyer's premium.' The catalogue also contains details of acceptable forms of payment. At the fall of the hammer an immediate deposit is usually required, the balance payable within 24 hours. If the plan is to pay by cash there may be a cash limit. Some auctions will accept payment by debit card. Sometimes credit or charge cards are acceptable, but will often incur an extra charge. A bank draft or bank transfer will have to be arranged in advance with your own bank as well as with the auction house. No car will be released before all payments are cleared. If delays occur in payment transfers then storage costs can accrue.

Buyer's premium
A buyer's premium will be added to the hammer price: don't forget this in your calculations. It is not unusual for there to be a further state tax or local tax on the purchase price and/or on the buyer's premium.

Viewing
In some instances it's possible to view on the day, or days before, as well as in the hours prior to, the auction. There are auction officials available who are willing to help out by opening engine and luggage compartments and to allow you to inspect the interior. While the officials may start the engine for you, a test drive is out of the question. Crawling under and around the car as much as you want is permitted, but you can't suggest that the car you are interested in be jacked up, or attempt to do the job yourself. You can also ask to see any documentation available.

Bidding

Before you take part in the auction, decide your maximum bid – and stick to it!

It may take a while for the auctioneer to reach the lot you are interested in, so use that time to observe how other bidders behave. When it's the turn of your car, attract the auctioneer's attention and make an early bid. The auctioneer will then look to you for a reaction every time another bid is made, usually the bids will be in fixed increments until the bidding slows, when smaller increments will often be accepted before the hammer falls. If you want to withdraw from the bidding, make sure the auctioneer understands your intentions – a vigorous shake of the head when he or she looks to you for the next bid should do the trick! Assuming that you are the successful bidder, the auctioneer will note your card or paddle number, and from that moment on you will be responsible for the vehicle. If the car is unsold, either because it failed to reach the reserve or because there was little interest, it may be possible to negotiate with the owner, via the auctioneers, after the sale is over.

Successful bid

There are two more items to think about. How to get the car home, and insurance. If you can't drive the car, your own or a hired trailer is one way, another is to have the vehicle shipped using the facilities of a local company. The auction house will also have details of companies specialising in the transfer of cars.

Insurance for immediate cover can usually be purchased on site, but it may be more cost-effective to make arrangements with your own insurance company in advance, and then call to confirm the full details.

eBay & other online auctions?

eBay & other online auctions could land you a car at a bargain price, though you'd be foolhardy to bid without examining the car first, something most vendors encourage. A useful feature of eBay is that the geographical location of the car is shown, so you can narrow your choices to those within a realistic radius of home. Be prepared to be outbid in the last few moments of the auction. Remember, your bid is binding and that it will be very, very difficult to get restitution in the case of a crooked vendor fleecing you – caveat emptor!

Be aware that some cars offered for sale in online auctions are 'ghost' cars. Don't part with any cash without being sure that the vehicle does actually exist and is as described (usually pre-bidding inspection is possible).

Auctioneers

Barrett-Jackson www.barrett-jackson.com; **Bonhams** www.bonhams.com; **British Car Auctions (BCA)** www.bca-europe.com or www.british-car-auctions.co.uk; **Christies** www.christies.com; **Coys** www.coys.co.uk; **eBay** www.eBay.com or www.eBay.co.uk; **H&H** www.handh.co.uk; **Mecum Auctions** www.mecum.com; **RM Sotheby's** www.rmsothebys.com; **Shannons** www.shannons.com.au; **Silver** www.silverauctions.com;

11 Paperwork
– correct documentation is essential!

The paper trail
Classic, collector and prestige cars usually come with a large portfolio of paperwork accumulated and passed on by a succession of proud owners. This documentation represents the real history of the car, and from it can be deduced the level of care the car has received, how much it's been used, which specialists have worked on it and the dates of major repairs and restorations. All of this information will be priceless to you as the new owner, so be very wary of cars with little paperwork to support their claimed history.

Registration documents
All countries/states have some form of registration for private vehicles whether its like the American title system or the British 'log book' system.

It is essential to check that the registration document is genuine. In the UK the current (Euro-aligned) registration document is named 'V5C,' and is printed in coloured sections of blue, green and pink. The blue section relates to the car specification, the green section has details of the new owner and the pink section is sent to the DVLA in the UK when the car is sold. A small section in yellow deals with selling the car within the motor trade. In the UK the DVLA will provide details of earlier keepers of the vehicle upon payment of a small fee, and much can be learned in this way. In the US and other countries, this information sharing is not allowed. If the car has a foreign registration there may be expensive and time-consuming formalities to complete. Do you really want the hassle?

Roadworthiness certificate
Most country/state administrations require that vehicles are regularly tested to prove that they are safe to use on the public highway and do not produce excessive emissions. In the UK that test (the 'MoT') is carried out at approved testing stations, for a fee. In the USA the requirement varies, some states insist on an emissions test every two years as a minimum, while the police are charged with pulling over unsafe-looking vehicles. Cars as old as 356s are generally exempt.

In the UK the test is required on an annual basis once a vehicle becomes three years old. Of particular relevance for older cars is that the certificate issued includes the mileage reading recorded at the test date and, therefore, becomes an independent record of that car's history. Ask the seller if previous certificates are available. Without an MoT the vehicle should be trailered to its new home, unless you insist that a valid MoT is part of the deal. (Not such a bad idea this, as at least you will know the car was roadworthy on the day it was tested and you don't need to wait for the old certificate to expire before having the test done.)

Road licence
The administration of every country/state charges some kind of tax for the use of its road system. The actual form of the 'road licence,' and how it is displayed, varies enormously country to country and state to state.

Whatever the form of the 'road licence,' it must relate to the vehicle carrying it and must be present and valid if the car is to be driven on the public highway. The value of the license will depend on the length of time it will continue to be valid. In the UK, if a car is untaxed because it has not been used for a period of time, the owner has to inform the licensing authorities. Otherwise, the vehicle's date-related registration number will be lost and there will be a painful amount of paperwork to get it re-registered. Also in the UK, vehicles built before the end of 1972 are provided with 'tax discs' free of charge, but they must still display a valid disc. Car clubs can often provide formal proof that a particular car qualifies for this valuable concession.

Certificates of Authenticity

Porsche provides a Certificate of Authenticity (CoA) proving the age and authenticity (e.g. engine and chassis numbers, paint colour and trim) of a particular vehicle. If the owner has one of these it is a definite bonus. To obtain one, the Porsche importer/distributor in your country is the best starting point.

If the car has been used in European classic car rallies it may have a FIVA (Federation Internationale des Vehicules Anciens) certificate. The so-called 'FIVA Passport,' or 'FIVA Vehicle Identity Card,' enables organisers and participants to recognise whether or not a particular vehicle is suitable for individual events. If you want to obtain such a certificate go to www.fbhvc.co.uk or www.fiva.org. There will be similar organisations in other countries, too.

Valuation certificate

Hopefully, the vendor will have a recent valuation certificate, or letter signed by a recognised expert stating how much he, or she, believes the particular car to be worth (such documents, together with photos, are usually needed to get 'agreed value' insurance). The easiest way to find out how to obtain a formal valuation is to contact the owners club.

Service history

Try to obtain as much service history and other paperwork pertaining to the car as you can. Naturally, dealer stamps, or specialist garage receipts score most points in the value stakes. However, anything helps in the great authenticity game, items like the original bill of sale, handbook, parts invoices and repair bills, adding to the story and the character of the car. Even a brochure correct to the year of the car's manufacture is a useful document and something that you could well have to search hard to locate in future years. If the seller claims that the car has been restored, then expect receipts and other evidence from a specialist restorer.

If the seller claims to have carried out regular servicing, ask what work was completed, when, and seek some evidence of it being carried out. Your assessment of the car's overall condition should tell you whether the seller's claims are genuine.

Restoration photographs

If the seller tells you that the car has been restored, then expect to be shown a series of photographs taken while the restoration was under way. Pictures taken at various stages, and from various angles, should help you gauge the thoroughness of the work. If you buy the car, ask if you can have all the photographs as they form an important part of the vehicle's history. It's surprising how many sellers are happy to part with their car and accept your cash, but want to hang on to their photographs! In the latter event, you may be able to persuade the vendor to get a set of copies made.

12 What's it worth?
– let your head rule your heart

Condition

If the car you've been looking at is really bad, then you've probably not bothered to use the marking system in chapter 9 – 60 minute evaluation. You may not even have got as far as reading that chapter at all!

If you did use the marking system in chapter 9 you'll know whether the car is in Excellent (maybe Concours), Good, Average or Poor condition or, perhaps, somewhere in-between these categories.

Many classic/collector car magazines run a regular price guide. If you haven't bought the latest editions, do so now and compare their suggested values for the model you are thinking of buying: also look at the auction prices they're reporting. Values have been fairly stable for some time, but some models will always be more sought-after than others. Trends can change too. The values published in the magazines tend to vary from one magazine to another, as do their scales of condition, so read carefully the guidance notes they provide. Bear in mind that a car that is truly a recent show winner could be worth more than the highest scale published. Assuming that the car you have in mind is not in show/concours condition, then relate the level of condition that you judge the car to be in with the appropriate guide price. How does the figure compare with the asking price? Before you start haggling with the seller, consider what effect any variation from standard specification might have on the car's value. If buying from a dealer, remember there will be a dealer's premium on the price.

Desirable options/extras

In general, prices are determined by year and model. Within each, the more powerful engines specification always adds to the price. Period options when listed on the CoA help increase the price a little, though often the CoAs have partial or no options listed. Coupes fitted with factory sunroofs always command a premium compared to those without.

Undesirable features

Anything non-authentic to original build specification detracts from the value. The exception to this is the Outlaw 356. These are mild to radical customs often fitted with performance enhancements. If this is what you're looking for, you need to have the same taste as the creator.

Mechanical troubles are far less a concern than poor quality restoration work and missing or incorrect parts.

Over-restored: in this case it probably isn't better than original fit and finish, but rather things chrome-plated that shouldn't be, updated but incorrect mechanicals, and things that conflict with the CoA. Inflated asking price says 'Go away.'

Striking a deal

Negotiate on the basis of your condition assessment, mileage, and fault rectification cost. Also take into account the car's specification. Be realistic about the value, but don't be completely intractable: a small compromise on the part of the vendor or buyer will often facilitate a deal at little real cost.

13 Do you really want to restore?
– it'll take longer and cost more than you think

First, go back to Chapter 2 and read the bit about structural repair and paint cost. Okay, now read on.

While there are probably some rust-free unrestored 356s out there, please be assured there aren't very many. Most were restored years ago and have now become second-generation projects. These are really scary, because you don't know how it was restored the first time, when the value of a 356 was much lower. You can price out the component pieces, and (if you have a famous television series) ignore the price of labour and you'll do just fine.

In reality the market price of the top quality finished car determines the value of those in lesser condition. This price nearly always is greater than can be justified for the work needing to be done. The only way of avoiding this is to buy the car before the market recognizes the potential value of the car. You'll need Mr Peabody for that, because the market is pretty good at anticipating these days.

Restoring a family owned car is a sentimental way to justify the same ill-advised decision. It will still cost the same, but it is Uncle Fred's car and you saved it. If you don't have to actually buy the car, it might actually work out better than expected. Isn't it a shame though, that Uncle Fred bought a Karmann Hardtop instead of a Carrera 2 cabriolet?

If you are planning to do the work yourself and the car has 'typical rust,' you'd better be a competent welder. Remember that this is a unit body car and open cars are prone to distortion due to their inherent weakness. Even with a rotisserie (yes, you can make one of those too), experts would still do it on a chassis jig. You might also want to pick up a copy of Jim Kellogg's DIY 356 restoration book before embarking. If you're still game, have at it. If not, that's okay, you can always resell it on eBay.

Accident damaged cars are generally beyond the scope of most and can be worth more in component parts. The latter is not often the case these days. If it was a sound car to start with, it could be easier and more economical to repair than a 'typical rust' car. It is a risky proposition though, if you aren't in the body repair business.

You've probably heard this before, but the only logical way to approach purchasing a 356 is to buy the best one you can afford. If you can only afford a 356 restoration project, then buy the best Pontiac Fiero you can afford. You'll be happier – especially if the market picks up on Fieros.

Paint faults generally occur due lack of protection/maintenance, or to poor preparation prior to a respray or touch-up. Some of the following conditions may be present in the car you're looking at:

Orange peel
This appears as an uneven paint surface, similar to the appearance of the skin of an orange. The fault is caused by the failure of atomized paint droplets to flow into each other when they hit the surface. It's sometimes possible to rub out the effect with proprietary paint cutting/rubbing compound or very fine grades of abrasive paper. A respray may be necessary in severe cases. Consult a bodywork repairer/paint shop for advice on the particular car.

Cracking
Severe cases are likely to have been caused by too heavy an application of paint (or filler beneath the paint). Also, insufficient stirring of the paint before application can lead to the components being improperly mixed, and cracking can result. Incompatibility with the paint already on the panel can have a similar effect. To rectify the problem it is necessary to rub down to a smooth, sound finish before respraying the problem area.

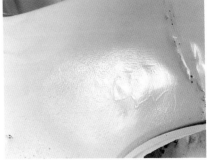

Orange peel and runs are the hallmarks of poor painters.

Crazing
Sometimes the paint takes on a crazed rather than a cracked appearance when the problems mentioned under 'Cracking' are present. This problem can also be caused by a reaction between the underlying surface and the paint. Paint removal and respraying the problem area is usually the only solution.

Blistering
Almost always caused by corrosion of the metal beneath the paint. Usually perforation will be found in the metal and the damage will usually be worse than that suggested by the area of blistering. The metal will have to be repaired before repainting.

Micro blistering
Usually the result of an economy respray where inadequate heating has allowed moisture to settle on the car

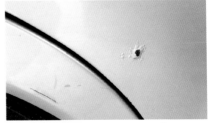

Cracks and blisters always have something unpleasant beneath the painted surface.

before spraying. Consult a paint specialist, but usually damaged paint will have to be removed before partial or full respraying. Can also be caused by car covers that don't 'breathe.'

Fading
Some colours, especially reds, are prone to fading if subjected to strong sunlight for long periods without the benefit of polish protection. Sometimes proprietary paint restorers and/or paint cutting/rubbing compounds will retrieve the situation. Often a respray is the only real solution.

Peeling
Often a problem with metallic paintwork when the sealing lacquer becomes damaged and begins to peel off. Poorly applied paint may also peel. The remedy is to strip and start again!

Peeling paint indicates poor surface preparation, too many paint layers, or both.

Dimples
Dimples (fisheyes) in the paintwork are caused by the residue of polish (particularly silicone types) or oil not being removed properly before respraying. Paint removal and repainting is the only solution.

Dents
Small dents are usually easily cured by the 'Dentmaster,' or paintless dent removal, that sucks or pushes out the dent (as long as the paint surface is still intact). Companies offering dent removal services usually come to your home: consult your telephone directory.

15 Problems due to lack of use

– just like their owners, Porsche 356s need exercise

Cars, like humans, are at their most efficient if they exercise regularly. A run of at least ten miles, once a week, is recommended for classics.

Seized components

Pistons in brake calipers and master cylinders can seize. The clutch may seize if the plate becomes stuck to the flywheel because of corrosion. Handbrakes (parking brakes) can seize if the cables and linkages rust. Pistons can seize in the bores due to corrosion.

Put a little gas in the tank and fire her up? Probably not a good idea ...

Fluids

Old, acidic oil can corrode bearings. Silt settling and solidifying can cause overheating. Brake fluid absorbs water from the atmosphere and should be renewed every two years. Old fluid with a high water content can cause corrosion and pistons/calipers to seize (freeze) and can cause brake failure when the water turns to vapour near hot braking components.

A gearbox that looks like this is asking to be rebuilt.

Tyre problems

Tyres that have had the weight of the car on them in a single position for some time will develop flat spots, resulting in some (usually temporary) vibration. The tyre walls may have cracks or (blister-type) bulges, meaning new tyres are needed.

Shock absorbers (dampers)

With lack of use, the dampers will lose their elasticity or even seize. Creaking, groaning and stiff suspension are signs of this problem.

This delightfully crusty aftermarket exhaust will require a little heat to remove.

Rubber and plastic

Window and door seals can harden and leak. Boots can crack. Wiper blades will harden.

Electrics

The battery will be of little use if uncharged for many months. Earthing/grounding problems are common when the connections have corroded. Old bullet and spade type electrical connectors commonly rust/corrode and require disconnection, cleaning, and protection (eg Vaseline). Sparkplug electrodes often corrode in an unused engine. Wiring insulation can harden and fail.

Rotting exhaust system

Exhaust gas contains a high water content, so exhaust systems corrode very quickly from the inside when the car is not used.

16 The Community
– key people, organisations and companies in the 356 world

Books

Porsche: Excellence was Expected, by Karl Ludvigsen – the definitive Porsche history, albeit a little pricey. All of the 356 content is in Volume 1 (of 3). Older single volume editions are nearly as good. Published by Bentley Publishers, ISBN: 978-0-83760235-6

The Book of Porsche 356, by Brian Long – a thorough history of the 356 production cars, largely illustrated with period images, many in colour. Included are some period racing versions and a chapter on replicas. Published by Veloce Publishing Limited, ISBN: 978-1-84584035-8-6

Porsche Technical Manual, by Henry Elfink – an older (1969) aftermarket repair manual. Not up to the factory workshop manual quality, but considerably less expensive. Available on eBay and used book stores. Published by Lash International Inc, ISBN: 978-0-90185800-9

356 Porsche Technical and Restoration Guide, by 356 Registry editors and members – an older (1974-1993) compilation of technical articles originally published in the club magazine. Published by Beeman Jorgensen, Inc., ISBN: 978-0-92975810-7

Porsche 356, Guide to Do-It-Yourself Restoration, by Jim Kellogg – the second edition of this book. If you think you want to take on a project, read this first. Published by Beeman Jorgensen, Inc, ISBN: 978-0-92975826-8

The 356 Porsche, A Restorer's Guide to Authenticity, by Dr Brett Johnson – the third edition of the authenticity book. Earlier editions are less complete. A fourth edition is anticipated. Published by Beeman Jorgensen, Inc, ISBN: 978-0-92975816-9

Clubs

Clubs are by far the best resource for information and feedback on vendors, as well a potential source of vehicles. The best place to start is the US-based 356 Registry, which is not actually a registry, but is by far the oldest and largest of these groups, founded in 1974 with around 7000 members from all over the world. The listing below is courtesy of the 356 Registry.

North American Clubs

The 356 Registry has the most comprehensive listing of clubs, restoration facilities, parts suppliers, dealers and just about anything you can imagine related to the 356. Most are US based, but there are numerous listings from other countries. There are around 30 non-affiliated regional US club listings. www.porsche356registry.org

Maple Leaf 356 Club of Canada
Mike Kieley
PO Box 220 – 10 River Bluff Path
Rockwood, ON Canada N0B 2K0
519-856-1232
mike@smartseniors.ca

Porsche Club Mexico A.C.
porscheclubmx@yahoo.com
www.porscheclubmexico.com.mx

European 356 Clubs
Porsche 356 Club Deutschland e.V.
Henk Schotanus, membership
Braeckweg 14, 6732 GA Harskamp
Netherlands
info@porsche356clubdeutschland.de
www.Porsche-356-Club-Deutschland.de

356 Register of Porsche Club Great
Britain
Fred Hampton
356@porscheclubgb.com

Registro Italiano Porsche 356
Roberto Bertaccini
www.registroitalianoporsche356.it

356 Porsche Club de France
Email 356@porscheclub.fr
http://356.typepad.fr

Porsche Classic Club Austria
office@porsche-classic-club.at

Porsche 356 Klubb, Sverige
Mikael Marin, Majvagen 25, S-167 52
Bromma, Sweden
www.porsche356klubb.se

Porsche Classic Club Luxembourg
paul.decker@education.lu

Porsche 356 Club Schweiz
Frank Baumann
www.porsche-356-club.ch

356 Stammtisch in South Germany
kontakt@356-stammtisch-mannheim.de

Porsche 356 Klubb Norge
Postboks 20 NO-3521 JEVNAKER
torf@mamut.com

Porsche 356 Club Nederland
Ton Vos, Chair. Henk Schotanus,
Member registration.
Postbus 356, 2660 AB Bergschenhoek,
Netherlands
clubblad@porsche356club.nl

Porsche Club Classic Belgium
info@porsche-classic-club.be

Porsche 356 Club Danmark
Vestergade 83, DK-8000 Arhus C
Freddie Eriksen
mogens.lumbye@porsche356.dk

Club Porsche 356 Espana
acasas@porsche-club356spain.com

Asia-Pacific Clubs
Australian Porsche 356 Register
PO Box 277
Port Melbourne, VIC 3207, Australia
www.356.com.au

356 Down Under
c/o Porsche Club NZ (INC)
PO Box 34-356
Birkenhead Auckland 0746
New Zealand
nz356downunder@xtra.co.nz
www.porsche.org.nz

Porsche 356 Club of Japan
356club@neko.co.jp

Africa
Porsche 356 Register of South Africa
peterd@carreramotors.co.za

17 Vital statistics

– essential data at your fingertips

Chassis number list

Chassis numbers can be misleading. The number indicates the order in which the chassis was constructed by individual coachbuilders, but not the order in which the car was completed or sold. Due to damage during assembly or component failures, cars many months out of sequence were completed and potentially fitted with trim and mechanical items that were used on later cars being finished alongside them. Cars built toward the end of a model year are frequently officially included in the next year's production figures. When a major change occurred, such as 356 to 356A, some unusual permutations were created. While these cars lead to confusion and controversy, it is not difficult to understand why they exist. It should be noted, however, that they are the exception; not the rule.

To further complicate matters, the list provided by Porsche is presented in calendar years, not model years. Most model changes transpired after the factory summer break, but in the early years, they are somewhat confusing. Prior to 1955, model changes are defined by the significant modifications delineated in the Porsche parts manuals.

Engine numbers are also a bit troubling for some of the same reasons listed above. The numbers on the list should be considered relative: this is especially true at the beginning and end of a model or calendar year. The only way to verify which engine was fitted to which chassis is to examine the original factory records. This service is provided to owners of 356s in the form of a Certificate of Authenticity by Porsche distributors in various countries, or by Porsche AG.

For years, the chassis number list that was contained in the *Porsche Specs* book was the gospel according to Porsche. In the early 1990s, with the help of Olaf Lang at Porsche AG, Wayne Stone and Marco Marinello, the following, more accurate list overleaf was compiled. It contains the several additional series of cars, Carrera engine types and exchange chassis numbers. It is interesting to note that some of the latter are duplicates of 1952 cabriolet numbers. A number of gaps in numerical series are not seen in the original Porsche list. Several typographical errors have been corrected, as well.

Year mfg	Vehicle and engine model designation		Engine model	Crank-case	Carbs	Stroke/ bore	Compr. ratio	HP (DIN) @ RPM	Engine serial #
1950	**(356)**	356/1100	369	2 PB	32 PBI	64/73.5	7:1	40 @ 4200	0101-0411
1951		356/1100	369	2 PB	32 PBI	64/73.5	7:1	40 @ 4200	0412-0999
									10001-10137
		356/1300	506	2 PB	32 PBI	64/80	6.5:1	44 @ 4200	1001-1099
									20001-20821
	from Oct.	356/1500	527	2 RB	40 PBIC	74/80	7:1	60 @ 5000	30001-30737
1952		356/1100	369	2 PB	32 PBI	64/73.5	7:1	40 @ 4200	10138-10151
		356/1300	506	2 PB	32 PBI	64/80	6.5:1	44 @ 4200	20822-21297
	until Nov.	356/1500	527	2 RB	40 PBIC	74/80	7:1	60 @ 5000	30738-30z750
	from Aug.	356/1500	546	2 PB	32 PBI	74/80	7:1	55 @ 4400	30751-31025
	from July	356/1500 S	528	2 RB	40 PBIC	74/80	8.2:1	70 @ 5000	40001-40117
1953		356/1100	369	2 PB	32 PBI	64/73.5	7:1	40 @ 4200	10152-10161
		356/1300	506	2 PB	32 PBI	64/80	6.5:1	44 @ 4200	21298-21636
		356/1500	546	2 PB	32 PBI	74/80	7:1	55 @ 4400	31026-32569
		356/1500 S	528	2 RB	40 PBIC	74/80	8.2:1	70 @ 5000	40118-40685
	from Sept.	356/1300 S	589	2 RB	32 PBI	74/74.5	8.2:1	60 @ 5500	50001-50017
1954		356/1100	369	2 PB	32 PBI	64/73.5	7:1	40 @ 4200	10162-10199
		356/1300	506	2 PB	32 PBI	64/80	6.5:1	44 @ 4200	21637-21780
	until Nov.	356/1300 S	589	2 RB	32 PBI	74/74.5	8.2:1	60 @ 5500	50018-50099
	July to Nov.	356/1300 A	506/1	2 PB	32 PBI	74/74.5	6.5:1	44 @ 4200	21781-21999
	until Dec.	356/1500	546	2 PB	32 PBI	74/80	7:1	55 @ 4400	32570-33899
	until Dec.	356/1500 S	528	2 RB	40 PICB	74/80	8.2:1	70 @ 5000	40686-40999
	From Nov.	356/1300	506/2	3 PB	32 PBI	74/74.5	6.5:1	44 @ 4200	22001-22021
	From Dec.	356/1300 S	589/2	3 RB	32 PBIC +	74/74.5	7.5:1	60 @ 5500	50101-50127
		356/1500	546/2	3 PB	32 PBI	74/80	7:1	55 @ 4400	33901-34119
		356/1500 S	528/2	3 RB	40 PICB	74/80	8.2:1	70 @ 5000	41001-41048
1955	until Oct.	356/1300	506/2	3 PB	32 PBI	74/74.5	6.5:1	44 @ 4200	22022-22245
		356/1300 S	589/2	3 RB	32 PBIC +	74/74.5	7.5:1	60 @ 5500	50101-50127
	from July	Carrera 1500	547	RB	40 PII-4	66/85	9.5:1	110 @ 6200	90001-90096
		356/1500	546/2	3 PB	32 PBI	74/80	7:1	55 @ 4400	34120-35790
		356/1500 S	528/2	3 RB	40 PICB	74/80	8.2:1	70 @ 5000	41049-41999
	from Oct.	356A/1300	506/2	3 PB	32 PBI	74/74.5	6.5:1	44 @ 4200	22246-22273
	(356A)	356A/1300 S	589/2	3 RB	32 PBIC +	74/74.5	7.5:1	60 @ 5500	50128-50135
	from Nov.	Carrera 1500 GS	547/1	RB	40 PII-4	66/85	9:1	100 @ 6200	90501-90959
		Carrera 1500 GT	547/1	RB	40 PII-4	66/85	9:1	110 @ 6200	90501-90959
	from Oct.	356A/1600	616/1	3 PB	32 PBIC	74/82.5	7.5:1	60 @ 4500	60001-60608
	from Sept.	356A/1600 S	616/2	3 RB	40 PICB	74/82.5	8.5:1	75 @ 5000	80001-80110
1956		356A/1300	506/2	3 PB	32 PBI	74/74.5	6.5:1	44 @ 4200	22274-22471
		356A/1300 S	589/2	3 RB	32 PBIC +	74/74.5	7.5:1	60 @ 5500	50136-50155
		Carrera 1500 GS	547/1	RB	40 PII-4	66/85	9:1	100 @ 6200	90501-90959
		Carrera 1500 GT	547/1	RB	40 PII-4	66/85	9:1	110 @ 6200	90501-90959
		356A/1600	616/1	3 PB	32 PBIC	74/82.5	7.5:1	60 @ 4500	60609-63926
		356A/1600 S	616/2	3 RB	40 PICB	74/82.5	8.5:1	75 @ 5000	80111-80756

Reutter coupe	Karmann coupe	Karmann hardtop	Reutter cabriolet	Gläser cabriolet		Model years
5002-5013 5017-5018 5020-5026 5029-5032 5034-5104 5163-5410			5014-5015 5033 5115 5131	5001 5019 5027-5028 5105-5114 5116-5130		1950
5411-5600			5132-5138	5139-5162		
10531-11280			10001-10165	10351-10432		Model 51
11301-11360			10166-10211 10251-10270	10433-10469		
11361-11778			10271-10350 15001-15050	12301-12387		Model 52
11779-12084 50001-51231			15051-15116 60001-60394	The above two series include all America Roadsters		1953 Model
51232-52029			60395-60549			
52030-52844			60550-60693			1954 Model
52845-53008			60694-60722			1955 Model
53009-54223			60723-60923			
55001-55390			61001-61069			
55391-58311			61070-61499			

Year mfg	Vehicle and engine model designation		Engine model	Crank-case	Carbs	Stroke/bore	Compr. ratio	HP (DIN) @ RPM	Engine serial #
1957	until Aug.	356A/1300	506/2	3 PB	32 PBI	74/74.5	6.5:1	44 @ 4200	22472-22999
		356A/1300 S	589/2	3 RB	32 PBIC +	74/74.5	7.5:1	60 @ 5500	50156-50999
		Carrera 1500 GS	547/1	RB	40 PII-4	66/85	9:1	100 @ 6200	90501-90959
		Carrera 1500 GT	547/1	RB	40 PII-4	66/85	9:1	110 @ 6200	90501-90959
		356A/1600	616/1	3 PB	32 PBIC	74/82.5	7.5:1	60 @ 4500	63927-66999
		356A/1600S	616/2	3 RB	40 PICB	74/82.5	8.5:1	75 @ 5000	80757-81199
	from Sept. (356A T 2)	Carrera 1500 GS	547/1	RB	40 PII-4	66/85	9:1	100 @ 6200	90501-90959
		Carrera 1500 GT	547/1	RB	40 PII-4	66/85	9:1	110 @ 6200	90501-90959
		356A/1600	616/1	3 PB	32 NDIX	74/82.5	7.5:1	60 @ 4500	67001-68216
		356A/1600 S	616/2	3 PB	32 NDIX	74/82.5	8.5:1	75 @ 5000	81201-81521
1958		356A/1600	616/1	3 PB	32 NDIX	74/82.5	7.5:1	60 @ 4500	68217-72468
		356A/1600 S	616/2	3 PB	32 NDIX	74/82.5	8.5:1	75 @ 5000	81522-83145
	from May	Carrera 1500 GT	692/0	RB	40 PII-4	66/85	9:1	110 @ 6400	91001-91037
			692/1	PB	40 PII-4	66/85	9:1	110 @ 6400	92001-92014
	from Aug.	Carrera 1600 GS	692/2	PB	40 PII-4	66/87.5	9.5:1	105 @ 6500	93001-93065
1959	from Feb.	Carrera 1600 GT	692/3	PB	W 40 DCM	66/87.5	9.8:1	115 @ 6500	95001-95114
	until Sept.	356A/1600	616/1	3 PB	32 NDIX	74/82.5	7.5:1	60 @ 4500	72469-79999
		356A/1600 S	616/2	3 PB	32 NDIX	74/82.5	8.5:1	75 @ 5000	83146 -84770
	from Sept. (356B T 5)	356B/1600	616/1	3 PB	32 NDIX	74/82.5	7.5:1	60 @ 4500	600101-601500
		356B/1600 S	616/2	3 PB	32 NDIX	74/82.5	8.5:1	75 @ 5000	84771-85550
		356B/1600 S-90	616/7	3 PB	40 PII-4	74/82.5	9:1	90 @ 5500	800101-802000
		Carrera 1600 GS	692/2	PB	40 PII-4	66/87.5	9.5:1	105 @ 6500	93101-93138
		Carrera 1600 GT	692/3	PB	W 40 DCM	66/87.5	9.8:1	115 @ 6500	95001-95114
1960		356B/1600	616/1	3 PB	32 NDIX	74/82.5	7.5:1	60 @ 4500	601501-604700
		356B/1600 S	616/2	3 PB	32 NDIX	74/82.5	8.5:1	75 @ 5000	85551-88320
		356B/1600 S-90	616/7	3 PB	40 PII-4	74/82.5	9:1	90 @ 5500	800101-802000
		Carrera 1600 GT	692/3	PB	W 40 DCM	66/87.5	9.8:1	115 @ 6500	95001-95114
			692/3A	PB	44 PII-4	66/87.5	9.8:1	134 @ 7300	96001-96050
1961	until Sept.	356B/1600	616/1	3 PB	32 NDIX	74/82.5	7.5:1	60 @ 4500	604701-606799
		356B/1600 S	616/2	3 PB	32 NDIX	74/82.5	8.5:1	75 @ 5000	88321-89999 / 085001-085670
		356B/1600 S-90	616/7	3 PB	40 PII-4	74/82.5	9:1	90 @ 5500	802001-803999
		Carrera 1600 GT	692/3A	PB	44 PII-4	66/87.5	9.8:1	134 @ 7300	96001-96050
	from Sept. from Aug. (356B T 6)	356B/1600	616/1	3 PB	32 NDIX	74/82.5	7.5:1	60 @ 4500	606801-607750
		356B/1600 S	616/12	3 PB	32 NDIX	74/82.5	8.5:1	75 @ 5000	700001-701200
		356B/1600 S-90	616/7	3 PB	40 PII-4	74/82.5	9:1	90 @ 5500	804001-804630
1962	until July	356B/1600	616/1	3 PB	32 NDIX	74/82.5	7.5:1	60 @ 4500	607751-608900
		356B/1600 S	616/12	3 PB	32 NDIX	74/82.5	8.5:1	75 @ 5000	701201-702800
		356B/1600 S-90	616/7	3 PB	40 PII-4	74/82.5	9:1	90 @ 5500	804631-805600
		Carrera 2/2000 GS	587/1	PB	40 PII-4	74/92	9.2:1	130 @ 6200	97001-97446
	from July	356B/1600	616/1	3 PB	32 NDIX	74/82.5	7.5:1	60 @ 4500	608901-610000
		356B/1600 S	616/12	3 PB	32 NDIX	74/82.5	8.5:1	75 @ 5000	702801-705050
		356B/1600 S-90	616/7	3 PB	40 PII-4	74/82.5	9:1	90 @ 5500	805601-806600

Reutter coupe	Karmann coupe	Karmann hardtop	Reutter cabriolet	Gläser cabriolet	Speedster	Convertible D	Roadster
58312-59099 100001-101692			61500-61892		83201-83791		
101693-102504			150001-150149		83792-84370		
102505-106174			150150-151531		84371-84922	85501-85886	
106175-108917			151532-152475		84923-84954	85887-86830	
108918-110237			152476-152943				86831-87391
110238-114650			152944-154560				87392-88920
114651-117476		200001-201048	154561-155569				88921-89010 Drauz 89011-89483 D'leteren
117601-118950		201601-202200	155601-156200				89601-89849
118951-121099	210001-210899	202201-202299	156201-156999				
121100-123042	210900-212171		157000-157768				

Year mfg	Vehicle and engine model designation		Engine model	Crank-case	Carbs	Stroke/ bore	Compr. Ratio	HP (DIN) @ RPM	Engine serial #
1963	until July	356B/1600	616/1	3 PB	32 NDIX	74/82.5	7.5:1	60 @ 4500	610001-611000
									0600501-0600600
									611001-611200*
		356B/1600 S	616/12	3 PB	32 NDIX	74/82.5	8.5:1	75 @ 5000	705051-706000
									0700501-0701200
									706001-707200*
		356B/1600 S-90	616/7	3 PB	40 PII-4	74/82.5	9:1	90 @ 5500	806601-807000
									0800501-0801000
									807001-807400*
		Carrera 2/2000 GS	587/1	PB	40 PII-4	74/92	9.2:1	130 @ 6200	97001-97446
		Carrera 2/2000 GT	587/2	PB	W 46 IDM/2	74/92	9.8:1	160 @ 6900	98001-98032
	from July **(356C)**	356C/1600 C	616/15	3 PB	32 NDIX	74/82.5	8.5:1	75 @ 5200	710001-711870
									730001-731102*
		356C/1600 SC	616/16	3 PB	40 PII-4	74/82.5	9.5:1	95 @ 5800	810001-811001
									820001-820522*
1964		356C/1600 C	616/15	3 PB	32 NDIX	74/82.5	8.5:1	75 @ 5200	711871-716804
									731103-733027*
		356C/1600 SC	616/16	3 PB	40 PII-4	74/82.5	9.5:1	95 @ 5800	811002-813562
									820523-821701*
		Carrera 2/2000 GS	587/1	PB	40 PII-4	74/92	9.2:1	130 @ 6200	97001-97446
1965		356C/1600 C	616/15	3 PB	32 NDIX	74/82.5	8.5:1	75 @ 5200	716805-717899
									733028-733197*
		356C/1600 SC	616/16	3 PB	40 PII-4	74/82.5	9.5:1	95 @ 5800	813563-813893
									821702-821855*
1966	March	356C/1600 SC	616/26	3 PB	40 PII-4	74/82.5	9.5:1	95 @ 5800	813894-813903

PB: Plain journal bearings
RB: Roller bearings

2: Two-piece crankcase
3: Three-piece crankcase

+ 589/2 1300S engines were also equipped with 40 PICB carburettors

* equipped with new heater system

Reutter coupe	Karmann coupe		Reutter cabriolet			
123043-125246	212172-214400		157769-158700			
126001-128104	215001-216738		159001-159832			
128105-131927	216739-221482		159833-161577			
131928-131930	221483-222580		161578-162165			
			162166-162175			

	Years mfg.	Chassis number
Additionally there were three series of exchange chassis for various cars, including race cars, prototypes, damaged customer cars, Abarth vehicles, South African built cabriolets and random production cars. These numbers do not correlate to any particular model or type.	1953-1961 1958-1962 1959-1965	12201-12376 5601-5624 13001-13414

Index

356 12
356A 12, 13
356B 13, 14
356C 14

Auctions 46, 47
Authenticity 3, 16, 17, 26

Barn finds 3
Basket case 26, 51
Battery 22, 30, 41, 42, 44, 54
Body repair 9
Books 9, 19, 55
Brakes 8-10, 12-14, 25, 38, 43, 45, 54
Bumpers 13, 29

Cabriolet 12-14
Carburettors 8, 9, 42
Carpet 24, 34
Carrera 12-14
Carrera 2 14
Certificate of Authenticity (CoA) 16, 24, 26, 30, 49, 57
Chassis 9, 24
Chassis number (VIN) 23, 40, 57-63
Clubs 55, 56
Clutch 8, 25, 43, 45
Convertible D 12, 13
Convertible top 29, 30
Coupe 12-14
Crash damage 31, 51

D'Ieteren 14, 22
Dashboard 25, 38
Doors 21, 23, 28, 36, 37
Driving 6, 10, 11, 44, 45

Engine 8, 25, 26, 54
Engine compartment 23, 24, 42, 43
Exhaust 44, 54

Exterior trim 31

Fender 21-23
Floor mats 34, 35
Front lid and hinges 22, 28
Front suspension 8, 25, 43
Fuel 6, 18
Fuel tank 39, 40
Fuel valve 25
Fuse block/cover 41

Gaps 21, 28
Gearbox 8, 10, 43
Gläser 12
Glass 32

Hardtop 29, 30
Headliner 25, 30, 35
Hubcaps 33

Instruments 38
Insurance 7, 18, 47
Interior 5, 9, 24, 25, 33-39

Jack 41

Kardex 16
Karmann 13, 14
Karmann hardtop 13, 14

Lead 21
Leaks 25, 43
Lights 9, 11, 32
Luggage area 6, 22, 23, 39-42

Manuals 9
Matching numbers 17
Mechanical repair 8
Mirror 31, 36

OEM 7
Outlaws 3, 17, 50

Paint 9, 21, 28, 52, 53

Parts 7-9
Pedals 25, 38
Porsche crest 31, 37
Pre-purchase inspection (PPI) 18
Prices 8, 9, 15
Project car 3, 26, 51

Rear lid 23, 24, 28
Recaro 14
Reutter 12, 14
Roadster 13, 14
Rubber seals 31, 54
Rust 9, 21, 24, 30, 39

Seals 31, 54
Seats 33, 34
Soft top 29, 30
Speedster 12, 34
Steering 10, 13, 25, 45
Steering wheel 37, 38
Structural repair 9
Suspension 9, 13, 25, 43, 54

T 2 13
T 5 13
T 6 13
Tonneau cover 30
Tools 41
Top boot 30
Trim 31
Tyres 11, 25, 33, 54

Upholstery (see interior)

Visors 35, 36

Wheels 12-14, 25, 33, 41
Windows 32
Windshield (windscreen) washer 41
Wipers 32
Wiring 44, 54